ELISA HOEKSTRA

The Recipe to Elevated Consciousness

Transmuting pain into power to gain true inner peace

EliSabeth Hoekstra

Reviews

"The Recipe to Elevated Consciousness" is a motivational self-help book/memoir written by Elisabeth Hoekstra. Hoekstra draws from her own life and uses personal anecdotes to convey lessons on various aspects of the current human condition to help people lead peaceful and fulfilling lives. The book reveals Elisabeth's story in interview format with the second half providing alternative remedies to help readers reach higher levels of consciousness. A must read!"

-Daniel G. Amen, M.D.—Psychiatrist and 12x New York Times Bestselling Author, Founder of Amen Clinics

"This book is a MUST READ for anyone that needs inspiration and motivation! Elisabeth teaches us that regardless of what odds one is facing, with hard work and conscious effort, there is a way out. Stay Elevated."

-Billy Carson—CEO of 4biddenknowledge TV, 2x best-selling author, TV Host, and Billboard Artist

"Elisabeth is an intuitive soul of nature, a kindred spirit with an inspirational story of enlightenment that will kindle that fire inside and ignite the radiant love and happiness for oneself that can only come with living a life with an elevated consciousness. No matter who you are or where you are along the road of your life's journey, here is a guide that will serve you well!"

    -Clinton Ober—Author of Earthing, The most important health discovery ever!

"Having known Elisabeth since middle school, she has always had a quiet brilliance about her. I am so excited for her to share her story and for everyone to see the perseverance and dedication to a better life she has always striven towards regardless of the obstacles she has faced. "The Recipe to Elevated Consciousness" finally gives a look behind the curtain at the strength and resilience that propelled her to health and happiness."

    -Brittany Horne

"A MUST READ!! As a close friend of Elisabeth for 16 years and just reading her name on the cover brought me to tears. She has found her purpose and I am glad she is here and able to share "the recipe" for us all! As a Navy Veteran, I cannot stress Mental Health enough!! This book explains the true power of investing in yourself beyond physical appearance. Elisabeth's personal testimony and experience will surely make you a believer of your inner being that needs to be brought to life, NOT the person society has formed you to be!!"

    -Janell N. Griffin—Founder and Owner of Inner Battle Fitness LLC, Navy Veteran, and Mental Health Enthusiast

"Elisabeth has been a dear friend to me for almost ten years. In the time I have known her, I have witnessed a mind-boggling amount of personal growth in Elisabeth. Watching her grow into the person she is, has been inspiring and ultimately started me on my own journey to inner peace. I have learned so much from and with Elisabeth and it truly changed the trajectory of my life. I am grateful for her mentorship and the modalities found in this book that she has introduced me to over the years. I was able to take the resources and information she passionately shares and leverage those to make changes in myself and my life I never thought I would be able to. I am the happiest, healthiest, most empowered I have been in my entire life, and it is without a doubt attributed largely to her. This book will give you the information needed to change your life if you are willing to do the work! And her story will provide inspiration and show you that you can change your life, no matter where you are in your journey."

-Rebecca C

"I loved this book. Elisabeth shares her life's journey of discovering energy, love, connection, abundance, and gratitude to help you find yours. You owe it to yourself to read this book."

-Perry Nickelston D.C.—The Lymph Doc, Founder of Stop Chasing Pain, @stopchasingpain

"I've known Elisabeth since we were 15. Watching her over the years has been one hell of a roller coaster. We were so different from one another, and yet we connected in such a way that our bond couldn't be closer. She literally became my best friend, like a sister. Watching her go through so much trauma over the years was heartbreaking. Despite the pain she endured, she was strong—no matter how hard she fell, she got back up. To see her now is nothing short of amazing. *The Recipe to Elevated Consciousness* was really an eyeopener to how strong one could be. I truly enjoyed walking with her through life from her perspective and how hard she fought to overcome those challenges. *The Recipe to Elevated Consciousness* definitely teaches one not to give up on self. It motivates you and teaches strategies on how to change your life. If you're facing a hard time in life, read *The Recipe to Elevated Consciousness*; let Elisabeth be the one to show you how you, too, can overcome deep, debilitating traumas. Elisabeth, I'm proud of you."

-Love Jenay, @justjenay

"In a generation of hidden and frequent trauma, I respect Elisabeth's journey to find natural ways to heal and rise above it."

    -Jonathan McReynolds—Grammy award winning gospel artist, author, and adjunct professor at Columbia College

The Recipe to Elevated Consciousness

Transmuting pain into power to gain true inner peace

Elisabeth Hoekstra

Copyright © 2022 by Elisabeth Hoekstra

All rights reserved.

No part of this book may be reproduced in any form or by any electronic or mechanical means, including information storage and retrieval systems, without written permission from the author, except for the use of brief quotations in a book review.

First Edition

Library of Congress Control Number: 2022902105

ISBN: 978-0-578-36820-7

Although the author and publisher have made every effort to ensure that the information in this book was correct at press time, the author and publisher do not assume and hereby disclaim any liability to any party for any loss, damage, or disruption caused by errors or omissions, whether such errors or omissions result from negligence, accident, or any other cause. Likewise, the author and publisher assume no responsibility for any false information. No liability is assumed for damages that may result from the reading or use of the information contained within.

Publisher info:

4biddenknowledge Inc

business@4biddenknowledge.com

Cover art and design by Laura C. Cantu, @LauraCCantu

Cover photo by Treagen Kier, Treagenkierstudios.com, @treagenkierstudios1

Make up - Sydni Jones, @facesbysydnij

Hair - Charles Harrison, @blakthai

Dedication

I dedicate this book to the two most important people in my life, my mom and my son. Mom, you stayed by my side throughout everything I put myself through and what I put you through. It takes a special and EXTREMELY patient person to deal with the things I did when I was younger. You never once turned your back on me. You were always there as my saving grace when I needed it most. You stayed happy all the time with positive feedback for me when I would fall to my deepest, darkest moments. Without your love, support, and belief in me, I couldn't have made it through what I have and become who I am today. You are my rock. I love you more than any word can describe. Thank you.

To my son, right now, you are too young to understand all of this, but I hope when you grow into maturity, you'll read this and know I have made these radical changes in my life for you, because of you. If you had never come to me, I don't even want to know where my life would be right now. Judging from where my life was headed before you, I would probably be in jail, dead, or deeply addicted to drugs. You were the catalyst to my extreme life change. You were the motivation I *needed to begin facing my shadows, and you are the reason I continue to stay on the path I'm on now. On top of that, you have been right by my side, bio-hacking with me, since the age of three when you first brain trained. I can see how all these different techniques have benefited you throughout your short time on this Earth, which is magical for me to watch. I know I will continue to watch you grow and mature into an amazingly brilliant, emotionally intelligent, beautiful on the inside and out man. What is present will only grow as you grow, and you are ALL of those things. I love you to the end of the universe and back.*

Forward

What is the definition of the word "recipe"? According to the dictionary, the definition of recipe is a set of instructions for preparing a particular dish, including a list of the ingredients required. This is precisely why I absolutely love the work that Elisabeth Hoekstra put into this book. Elisabeth has literally given us an amazing recipe for obtaining an elevated consciousness. All of the ingredients that one would need to elevate themselves from their current state of being are thoughtfully laid out in this book.

After reading Elisabeth's book, I could not help but think of my father who also suffered from most of the same addictions and mental health issues during his life. As much as he wanted to raise himself from his condition, he could not. He suffered from abandonment, drug addiction, and a rebellious mindset. Though he tried hard, he didn't have the right recipe. I could only think how a book like this could have helped give him a real chance to live a meaningful and happy life.

We can travel into the past to conduct some existential detective work in order to understand how our experiences have shaped our reactions in the present. The founding father of psychoanalysis,

Sigmund Freud, stated that our mind is like an iceberg—only a small part of it is above the waterline, while the rest drifts in the murky depths of our unconscious. Only when we pull our darkest fears and desires into the light of the conscious mind, where we can examine them calmly and analytically, will they begin to lose their monstrosity and much of their influence. What we do not know consciously—the repressed—is the true "other" to genuine self-knowledge. Elisabeth Hoekstra skillfully takes us on a journey to rediscover who we really are. It is through this epiphany of self-knowledge that we can truly begin to understand our true nature and do the shadow work needed to climb out of the abyss.

I am excited and blessed to have written this foreword, and I know that readers of this book will obtain real life-changing value. *The Recipe to Elevated Consciousness* will make bio-hacking a household term.

Billy Carson
    4biddenknowledge Inc
    2645 Executive Park Dr
    Suite 419
    Weston, FL 33331
    http://4biddenknowledge.com

About the Author

Elisabeth Hoekstra's reputation proceeds her in the many industries she has graced with her talents. As a teenager, she got her start in the entertainment world, where she worked as a model and actor. Elisabeth appeared on nationally syndicated television programs, movies, music videos, and magazines.

Elisabeth started volunteering at the young age of ten, helping at nursing homes and feeding the homeless; but, during her first year in high school, a trip to Matamoros, Mexico, sparked her passion for philanthropy. There, she helped build orphanages for orphaned children in that community.

In her early twenties, she attended Davenport College for business management and marketing administration, but her schooling did not stop there. At Schoolcraft College, she received her baking and pastry certification. She subsequentially mastered the art there as a sous chef, serving under one of only six Master Pastry Chefs in the country. Elisabeth graduated from Schoolcraft College on the Dean's list with honors and worked at several prestigious venues during her culinary run, including Oakland Hills Country Club. In 2017, she helped open and operate an award-winning restaurant.

In addition to her culinary work, she donated her time and talent to organize and host charity events she named "Breaking Brunch". The success from the first Breaking Brunch gained so much popularity that the news picked up the story to help promote the second event. The proceeds from these events were donated to multiple nonprofits that support women and children with cancer.

In 2017, while expanding her entrepreneurial skills, Elisabeth earned her real estate license. In 2018, having been named exclusive real estate agent for a statewide campaign, she broke all records for securing the most offices in the shortest period.

She used the political connections she built in her time as a record-breaking real estate agent to lobby for change and bring awareness to the troubling water quality and infrastructure issues plaguing the Detroit school systems.

In addition to these successes, Elisabeth also contributed significantly to nonprofits that focus on children's health and education, both through hosting fundraisers and advocacy.

You can see the trend, regardless of where her work takes her, the inner passion that drives Elisabeth always points back to her desire to serve others.

Elisabeth's current focus on mental health and holistic modalities, and ultimately her decision to write her first book, came from a different, darker source of inspiration.

Intermingled with her successes are moments of deep personal trauma, a life lived in the shadows. She learned all too well the impact that unresolved trauma can have on the trajectory of your future and the power and effort it takes to overcome these issues. Part of her success is undoubtedly a direct result of her passion for learning.

Elisabeth decided to clean up her life and dedicated herself to learning everything she possibly could about mental health, trauma resolution, bio-hacking, the many holistic modalities, and the science behind them, which she used to address her trauma. Her ambition alone would not have been enough without all the inner work she completed over the past ten-plus years.

Elisabeth hopes that by sharing her unfiltered story, she will help others realize that no matter how bad things are or how you ended up where you are at now, there is ALWAYS hope.

> "I've always had a passion for helping people. My book will help readers to identify their inner strengths and capabilities. It will also provide education to rejuvenate them to accomplish their life and career goals while elevating their consciousness to a new level. I believe knowledge is infinite. Everyone should learn, read, and grab as much knowledge as they can,"
>
> -Elisabeth Hoekstra

Throughout her various careers, Elisabeth saw how stress takes a toll on people's mental and physical well-being; what she observed led her to work at a holistic wellness center. There, by applying her business knowledge and utilizing her connections formed during previous careers, she quickly became the company's President.

Her overall success story led to her current position as Director of Operations for the worldwide brand and TV network, 4biddenknowledge Inc. She now helps organize and grow 4biddenknowledge Inc., all while hosting her popular podcast, "Bio-Hack Your Best Life", alongside President/CEO of 4biddenknowledge, Billy Carson.

Although *The Recipe to Elevated Consciousness* is Elisabeth Hoekstra's first literary accomplishment, we expect many more great works in the future.

Follow Elisabeth on: Facebook, Twitter, Instagram, YouTube, TikTok, her Website, and 4biddenknowledge.

Scan this QR code for easy access to all of Elisabeth's social sharing.

Introduction

Elisabeth, our true-to-life heroin, lived parallel lives, one to be seen by the public as "successful", yet all while suffering from hidden addictions, unresolved trauma, and abusive relationships. Elisabeth dove into drugs and alcohol at the early age of eleven, which only got worse as she spiraled down into her traumatic teenage years. She had run-ins with the law, experienced living on her own at fourteen, and endured multiple instances of sexual abuse as she was always around men much older than her.

It did not get much better for Elisabeth when drugs really took hold of her life as she struggled to leave toxic and abusive relationships with drug dealers, all while showing to the public, a lavish lifestyle. After experiencing her first modality—brain training, at the age of nineteen, she found hope that maybe her life could be different.

It took another seven years for Elisabeth to really make the effort and follow the steps to change her life. Her saving grace, Elisabeth's son provided her the motivation to begin a new life free from illegal activities likely to land her in jail and put her son at risk of a life in foster care. She knew she had to create change to support her new

Introduction

baby, so she began her amazing journey of experimenting with bio-hacking.

Having already dipped in and out of using holistic modalities, Elisabeth hacked her health throughout her life but got serious about it in her late 20's. Since then, Elisabeth has used over fifty different holistic modalities to elevate her consciousness, optimize her physical body and mind, and align with her true Divine nature.

Elisabeth now lives a lavish life not only on the outside but within as well. She is finally at peace and feels whole, something she struggled to achieve her entire life.

Join Elisabeth's drama-filled, inspiring journey as Regina Meredith interviews her about her life story in the first half of the book. The story reveals how Elisabeth overcame trauma after trauma to discover and dive into bio-hacking her way to elevated consciousness, manifesting her best life, and inspiring others to do the same.

In the second half, Elisabeth goes deep into the different modalities she used, her experience with them, and the science behind each. She includes links for informative and trustworthy websites so you can do your own research on the suggested therapies.

In the section, The Many Adventures of Elisabeth Hoekstra, you will find links to even more personal support by Elisabeth that can help you, too, Bio-hack Your Way to Your Best Life!

The Interview

When I first met Billy and told him my story, he encouraged me to write a book to inspire others to conquer what I already had lived through. He told me that the world needed to know how I overcame so much.

As I contemplated telling my story, I realized I didn't know where to begin. Billy suggested calling our friend Regina and asking her if she would talk with me in the way only Regina can. I knew her deep questioning would help me reveal my own story, and I can't thank her enough for helping me bring it to these pages.

In this section of *The Recipe to Elevated Consciousness*, you'll journey with me from the beginning of my life to where I am now. You'll walk through the most important parts of my life, the events that took the biggest toll on my body and mind and experience them with me. I wanted to show my lowest points in detail so others going through, or have gone through, what I've experienced can relate and gain the confidence to begin changing as I did.

I did not write this so you can feel sorry for me; I wrote this for quite the opposite reason. I want to ignite that fire inside your soul that everyone innately has, but most have forgotten is there. Many

Elisabeth Hoekstra

people walk through their lives robotically existing, jumping from one task to another, never consciously experiencing life, only reacting to it. Action/reaction is no way to live. Each one of us was born with the power inside to create the exact life we want. The stress of our day-to-day lives plus the trauma everyone endures creates amnesia within our minds, and we forget the power we have within to live our best life.

I'm here to show you through all my trauma, all my drama, all of my mistakes, which I call lessons, and all of the loss I've experienced so that you can find your way back to that magical flame within. You can rid your mind and body of the compiled crap it's picked up just by being alive in our current time. Through shedding these layers, you will consciously start to bio-hack your best life. The power is within YOU.

Scan this QR code and watch the full interview video on 4biddenknowledge.com.

Chapter 1

The Unconscious Root of My Trauma

Regina Meredith: Hi, I'm Regina Meredith, here in Florida with Elisabeth Hoekstra, and she has an incredible story to tell. I mean, people have been through situations in life that they have found challenging and traumatic. Still, honestly, Elisabeth's entire life had that portfolio, and it really took until just a few years ago to figure out what was going on and turn it around. But the real hallmark of her life is her incredible will and stamina. Even in the lowest moments, she was still by day, trying to excel, improve herself, learn, develop new careers, and do the best she could, highly successful at everything. Really interesting story of dysfunction, living alongside function and hiding the dysfunction from the world. So, I'm happy to be here with you.

Elisabeth Hoekstra: Yeah, thank you so much for the great introduction. I appreciate you.

Regina Meredith: You're so welcome. So, let's start at the beginning of your life because it wasn't an ordinary one. It started in a rather rushed and dramatic way outside Seoul, Korea, right? When your mother, at a very young age, had a boyfriend and became pregnant. He took off for college, she's left with the baby, and an American family adopted you.

Elisabeth Hoekstra: Yes, exactly. I was adopted when I was three months old by an American family. I found out later, as my parents told me about my story, that my father never knew about me because he went off to college, and my birth mother ended up giving me up for adoption. At that time in Korea, to be a single mom was impossible.

Regina Meredith: Well, it's probably quite true.

Elisabeth Hoekstra: Yes. My American family adopted me at three months old and I started my journey. It's interesting, I did some regression work to connect back to the day I was born because I have always had this sense of abandonment; I get overly emotional when I feel I'm being abandoned. It's almost as if when I get in a fight with somebody and they walk away from me, my whole inside feels like I am going to drop through the ground. It's a painful feeling physically.

I always wanted to figure out why I had this constant feeling of pain every time I felt abandoned, and I related that back to the adoption. So, I did some regression work and some bodywork, and I regressed back to being in the womb of my mom. Halfway through the pregnancy, the stress hormones from the mother are able to cross through the placenta and be felt by the baby. So, I felt her stress, and I felt she was disgusted, or because of her situation, she didn't want me. She was overwhelmingly stressed out.

Regina Meredith: Well, imagine what her life would have been like had she tried to keep you. I mean, she must have been terrified.

Elisabeth Hoekstra: Exactly, and her being so young. Through the regression, I relived my own birth, and I remember coming out of the womb. I relived all of these emotions; that's the crazy thing about bodywork, you can clearly feel what you've been through by bringing up your unconscious memories. So, I was feeling all these emotions and I remember coming out of the womb, and all I wanted to do was look at my mom and have her hug me. I wanted to feel the love of the lady who gave birth to me, and I didn't get to see her, and I never saw her eyes—the nurses just took me away.

Regina Meredith: After you've been so deeply bonded in utero, you could feel every breath and every pulse of blood. You knew what she was talking about because you were more whole in terms of your higher understanding still at that point, right? You knew her thoughts, her feelings, and then, just to be taken away.

Elisabeth Hoekstra: That theft broke me from the minute I came into this dimension. It broke me. Imagine coming into this world and feeling abandoned and left alone; it was really hard, and I wasn't placed with a family immediately. I was monitored at an orphanage for the first few months of my life. Through my regression work, I knew the social interaction was zilch. The nurses, back then, didn't how important it was to bond or to have physical touch being so young. I was deprived of that contact.

But the interesting thing, my learning about this experience healed something in me. I could comprehend the beginning of my abandonment issues and attach those feelings to a known conscious memory.

Regina Meredith: You didn't know where it was coming from. You thought you were just broken. So now, at what, three months? You arrive in America with your family. Do you have any recollection from that period of life of how it felt by being held and treated like a daughter by someone?

Elisabeth Hoekstra: You know what? Unfortunately, I don't.

Regina Meredith: You don't know from that age; I just threw that one out there.

Elisabeth Hoekstra: Honestly, I never felt adopted because this was all I ever knew, which is why it was so confusing, this abandonment. The reason I had to do so much work and dig to figure out why I was this way was because I never even considered being adopted could be a trauma for me. I felt like my family was my family all the time. I had no conscious memory of being born the way I was or how my life was for the first three months.

Regina Meredith: They cared for you, educated you, and treated you well.

Elisabeth Hoekstra: Oh, yeah. They did the best they could; my parents are great people.

Chapter 2

Abandonment

Regina Meredith: Yeah, so, you had your family, what's this abandonment about? Okay. So, things didn't go smoothly, necessarily, even though they were wonderful parents. There were other people who were in your life, and one of them was male, and he began abusing you sexually, right, from quite a young age?

Elisabeth Hoekstra: Yes, during some regression work, EMDR, I remembered when the abuse started. I couldn't speak full sentences yet. I was probably about three. I didn't know what was going on. I remember it was like a game, and the abuser would play these games with me.

Regina Meredith: What kind of games? Just because other women are watching this, this might trigger some things because sexual abuse is far more rampant globally than anyone understands. It has been, historically. So, talk about the game.

Elisabeth Hoekstra: It was like doctor. "Let me see, let me touch, what does this do?" curiosity. I remember he actually told me his penis was a bottle and I should suck it. The play was a lot of touching and exploring, really.

I remember it carried on for quite a long time. I was in fifth grade watching a video about sexual abuse, and I was like, "Wow, that's happening to me". I realized, "Okay, this is wrong". And so, I went home that day, and said, "Dad can you make so and so, stop touching me?" And my dad responded, "Yeah." He didn't think anything of it; he thought I was talking about playing games. But from that day, he never touched me again.

Regina Meredith: Like playing tag or something.

Elisabeth Hoekstra: Yes, pretty much. I had no recollection of the events after that until later in life when I started getting these crazy dreams.

Regina Meredith: Wow, fifth grade, you're up to eleven years old. So, the abuse continued all that time.

Elisabeth Hoekstra: Yes. Off and on.

Regina Meredith: Now, did you have any sense at the time what was happening as a little kid that something wasn't right with this picture, or was it just like, he was telling you this is the fun stuff we do, and it's okay? So, just, 2,3,4,5,6,7,8-years-old, it all seems pretty normal.

Elisabeth Hoekstra: Yes, I thought life was supposed to be this way, and I had no thought it was something bad until I saw the sexual abuse video in fifth grade.

Regina Meredith: And then, what happened? Let's look at it two different ways because it's the psychological stuff. You didn't think it was bad because you were a little kid, and you were raised with it; basically, you were playing. Now, you find out it's bad, and you're eleven years old. Now, what's that do to your psyche?

Elisabeth Hoekstra: I think I blocked it out. I remember I got a kind of sinking feeling in my stomach when I was watching it on TV, I thought, "Oh".

It was very surprising because I love this person, and I didn't process it, I don't think, at the time. I think I just felt kind of sunk.

Regina Meredith: Did you feel betrayed then, suddenly by

The Recipe to Elevated Consciousness

them when that happened? And did you have any guilty feelings yourself? Like, what did you do? Or were you too young to process it that way?

Elisabeth Hoekstra: I think I was too young. I don't remember ever thinking about it again until I started getting weird dreams.

Regina Meredith: Okay. But what it did was it started sexualizing you at an inappropriate age.

Elisabeth Hoekstra: Yeah.

Regina Meredith: Okay, and that's so not cool because that sets you up for deep patterns for the rest of your life.

Chapter 3

Nightmares Exposing the Truth

Regina Meredith: Now, let's talk about when the dream/nightmares began and when you talked to your parents.

Elisabeth Hoekstra: When I was about thirteen years old, I started getting these crazy nightmares where I woke up sweating, and my heart was racing, I could hardly breathe, and it was from a man in my dreams, touching me. And so, I started to wonder; because they were so real, if I was messed up. I'm considering, "Am I jacked up? This is craziness". It started affecting my day-to-day life because my sleep was constantly disturbed. I woke up with panic attacks, basically.

So, I asked my parents if I could go see a psychologist or therapist or someone so I could try to figure out what was going on with me. They agreed, and I explained to the therapist about the dreams, and finally processed the real experience. I started getting flashes of memory during the session with the therapist. And I remember almost having a panic attack as I'm talking to her, because she said, "Oh, we need to alert the authorities right now, and I need to tell your parents right now," and my heart started racing in panic. I'm like, "No,

I can't". I'm trying to go somewhere to get help, and I'm trying to process and feel better—

Regina Meredith: And they were going to turn it into a bigger issue.

Elisabeth Hoekstra: Huge issue.

Regina Meredith: They believed you at that point.

Elisabeth Hoekstra: Well, they didn't know what to think; though, they did believe me after my abuser admitted to the abuse.

Regina Meredith: I see. When he came forward and said, "That's true; I used to do that".

Elisabeth Hoekstra: Yes.

Regina Meredith: So now, let's take a moment of pause before we go into what happened after, starting at twelve years old and on. Sex and sexual contact, sensuality, sexual pleasure must have started getting hardwired in with your sense of value and self-worth in the world because you loved this person. And that would have seemed to indicate he loved you back as a little kid. So now, sex becomes central to who you are, your identity, and how you get love.

Elisabeth Hoekstra: Yes, exactly. I remember in middle school, I would dress in really tight clothes, and my dad would get so mad at me. He would say to me, "Look at you; you look like a slut right now", and I'd call back, "What? I look good".

I remember always trying to use my body and my clothes and to try to get attention, and in middle school, I got very popular, so all the boys wanted me, and I was dating boys way older than me at an early age. I started my sexual activity at a pretty early age.

Regina Meredith: Yeah. Well, also, after the dreams, after this acknowledgment, you also started trying to self-soothe. So, let's talk about what happened there. After you found all this out, after the dreams, after everyone was acknowledged, it was on the table; you needed to numb yourself at the same time. And so, you start drinking by twelve, right?

Elisabeth Hoekstra: Yes. I think it was right around then.

Before then, before I even knew all this was happening, I remember, I would try to always do things to take my mind and body away from the way I was feeling. I think I even tried to start drinking before then. I remember when I was really young, I took some sage because I heard it was like weed, and I smoked it. From the earliest age, I was always trying to feel different than how I was naturally feeling. So, of course, I was trying to grab anything I could.

Regina Meredith: Well then, how were you, aside from the sexual abuse, how were you feeling in your world? What were you trying to numb yourself or blunt yourself from?

Elisabeth Hoekstra: I was an angry, angry child, but I was also happy at the same time. But I would have these terrible tantrums, where I banged my feet and my arms against the floor. My parents learned to leave me alone in my room until I calmed down. Which I now think was the wrong thing to do. I needed attention; I needed someone to hold me and tell me it was going to be okay, ya know, abandonment issues.

Regina Meredith: Absolutely. Well, now we know that we carry DNA from previous generations of our birth parents. You don't know what your mother had been through, and her mother and her mother in Korea. And so, these anger patterns and this frustration, and maybe, trying to, on one hand, be attractive and another, hide yourself and not feel yourself really coming from a genetic imprint from long ago and somewhere else in the world.

Elisabeth Hoekstra: I believe that is probably the case, too, because things triggered me deeply, and when you examine them you wonder, "Where did I get this trigger?" I've dug into all my triggers since.

Regina Meredith: Did you ever get to know your birth mother? Did you ever meet her?

Elisabeth Hoekstra: No.

Regina Meredith: So, you don't know anything about your lineage.

Chapter 4

Too Young to Party

Regina Meredith: So, good thing is, there's a lot of good therapy out there. So, let's talk about that. You actually drank until you had alcohol poisoning, throwing up, I mean, out of control, starting age at twelve, thirteen, going to parties, I assume, your social life, and at some point, along in here, your sex life probably began too.

Elisabeth Hoekstra: So early; I started sneaking out, I think, at second grade. I was sneaking out of my house, me and my friends, and we would toy with people's houses, do all the kid stuff. I remember I started partying between eleven and thirteen. I think it was during sixth grade I started partying with high school kids.

Regina Meredith: Oh my gosh, you were eleven.

Elisabeth Hoekstra: I started going to high school parties and, yeah, blackout drunk. By the time I was in 8th-9th grade I was going to college parties.

Regina Meredith: Why did they let you do that? Oh, obviously, they weren't people who were looking out for your best interest.

Elisabeth Hoekstra: No, they weren't. I was a cute kid, I think that—

Regina Meredith: You were a little kid.

Elisabeth Hoekstra: I was. And I see how really, really dysfunctional it was, now that I'm an adult and I look back on it, but I definitely remember going to high school parties and them giving me beers; I'd rollerblade over to a friend's house, and his older brother would be having a party, and I'd be there drinking, and I loved the way it made me feel. It made me feel alive and normal; I finally felt normal. So, any party I could get to I was there so I could get some alcohol.

Regina Meredith: It made you feel more free, maybe.

Elisabeth Hoekstra: Yeah, free. It made me almost feel whole. I always felt like I had some sort of emptiness inside. So, the alcohol filled that hole for a bit until it wore off.

Regina Meredith: Oh, sure. Now, let's move up to fourteen, right in there where you moved in with someone. How did that happen? How did your parents take that?

Elisabeth Hoekstra: Well, I was an awful child.

Regina Meredith: You said mean things; you were out of control.

Elisabeth Hoekstra: Yeah, I was out of control. I had zero respect for my mom, and my dad; Dad was really angry. He had a lot of anger issues, and he would blow up on us. And I picked up the behavior, and I would take it out on my mom and manipulate her, but my dad, I couldn't.

Regina Meredith: You couldn't go against dad.

Elisabeth Hoekstra: Right. But my mom, I would call her out of her name and just, you know, I was horrid. I hated them at that time; I just hated everything. So, I moved in with my high school sweetheart. It was him, his cousin, and his dad who was on drugs, and we moved into an apartment.

Regina Meredith: You said his dad was a crackhead.

Elisabeth Hoekstra: He smoked crack and I believe took pills.

Regina Meredith: And you were fourteen.

Elisabeth Hoekstra: Yes, I was fourteen. So, that's where I learned how to hustle because we lived in an apartment complex, and some guys a couple doors down were selling weed, so I learned how to sell weed. I also had my best friend, who was living a couple doors down, he was sixteen, and all of us would get together and go to college parties. I was really out of control, partying all the time, still going to school, but going to college parties.

Regina Meredith: And by this time, you experienced an actual rape.

Elisabeth Hoekstra: I did.

Regina Meredith: Not the kind of kid stuff that makes you feel creepy, but a real rape.

Elisabeth Hoekstra: Yes. I was at a college party really, really wasted drunk, and a popular guy that everyone knew took me in the back. I remember he was trying to have sex with me, and I was telling him, "No, I don't want to have sex with you, no". And I remember repeating, "No, no", and he started coming onto me. And my body completely shut down. I lay there, screaming on the inside, but nothing came out. I was completely frozen; I was like a doll.

I couldn't even get words out of my mouth. Which, by the way, is a protection mechanism and trauma response by your brain, to completely disassociate. I did this often in my life. A lot of women carry guilt from rape because they didn't do "more" to stop it. I am a prime example. I didn't heal that part of myself until I started understanding human biology, the nervous system and how it works.

I left the party and went back to the apartment. I told my boyfriend about it, and they got so angry, they went back to the college party and were going to beat him up, and I felt so bad. A feeling of remorse for my abuser overcame me, a feeling I picked up most likely from the child abuse. So, within my skewed perception of right and wrong, I didn't want this guy to get badly hurt because of me; I ended up warning him they were coming for him.

My ex found out I told the attacker and came back to the apartment, and then, him and his cousin blamed it on me. They got really mad at me, and they threw all my stuff outside in the rain, and I mean, everything was outside. That was an awful day.

Regina Meredith: How did your parents react? So, they're like, "Good, at least we don't have to deal with her day to day". They kind of had it with you. So now, this ends, now, Child Protective Services is notified at some point for potential foster care.

Elisabeth Hoekstra: They were when they found out about my other abuser.

Regina Meredith: Oh, I see, okay, that happened earlier. So now, you're fourteen, the gigs up, did you go back home?

Elisabeth Hoekstra: Yeah, I went back home after my boyfriend threw my stuff out into the mud.

Chapter 5

Kidnapped to Bootcamp

Regina Meredith: Now, your parents were looking at maybe boarding school or something for you, but you ended up in a weird situation. And I've heard this story a couple of other times, so I'd like you to share this part, which is they decided you needed a little more intensive behavior modification and development. And so, they sent you to a boot camp. Let's talk about what happened. How old were you?

Elisabeth Hoekstra: I think I was fifteen or sixteen at that time. I remember planning to sneak out to my boyfriend's house that night, and instead I thought, "No, I'm pretty tired, I'm just going to sleep here tonight, and I'll see him tomorrow". And I remember the lights coming on in the middle of the night, and I remember there was a really big man and a woman in suits, they were in black suits, and they hollered, "Get up!" and I was taken a back, "Excuse me, who's this?".

They were rough and grabbed me out of my bed, and I'm thinking, "What is happening?" I'm half asleep. I'm so confused, wondering "Get up and go where? Who are these people?" And then I glanced outside my door and my mom and my dad were standing there, and they're crying. All I could think was, "What the hell is going on? What is this? Who are these people?" My parents didn't say anything to me. My bags were already packed. The people in suits walked me straight to the car. I didn't get to say goodbye to anybody; they rushed me out of the house and brought me to the airport.

I'm bawling crying at this time, thinking, "I don't know what is going on; my parents are supposed to protect me". I'm being kidnapped, you know? So, I'm at the airport, and I'm trying to get away by any means possible. So, I go to the bathroom, and the suit-lady stands outside the bathroom door, and I remember there was an airport staff person somewhere in the bathroom, and I was bawling. She asked me, "What's going on? Are you okay?" I responded, "I'm not okay, I don't know what's happening," and I guess she might have talked to the suit-lady because nothing ever came out of that; I still got put on a plane.

Regina Meredith: The woman must have told her you were part of a program. So, you got on a plane. Okay, and you ended up somewhere.

Elisabeth Hoekstra: Yeah. I was dropped off in the middle of the woods in Ashville, North Carolina. I was so confused. My memory of this is all very choppy for me; I was in a cabin or something with these other kids that also didn't know what was going on. Everyone crying, screaming, and one of the girls there was bulimic, and she was throwing up in front of me, and all I could do was think, "This is weird. Where am I at?"

I'm surrounded by crying kids, I'm crying, and everyone's confused; and come to find out my parents sent me to a therapeutic boot camp.

I think I was out there for about forty-five days in the middle of the woods, and to get home there were five levels you had to pass.

I remember making mousetraps, and I had to eat an entire apple; that was how I passed the first couple levels.

We had to make fires, out of bow drills—two sticks, and we had to make fires with tinder bundle and a rock, blow it and make the fire. I crossed all these levels so quickly, within the first two weeks, because I just wanted to go home so bad. So, they didn't know what to do because no one had ever done this before; they started giving me ridiculous things to do, like, putting the mouse trap together with my toes. And I did that.

Regina Meredith: I mean, you're such a clever, powerful person in this tiny little package. Everybody underestimated you, including them.

Elisabeth Hoekstra: Yes. I was running through their tests, heckling, "Give me some more; come on, I want to go home". They ran out of stuff for me to do because I passed all the levels so quickly, so they sent me off for five days to camp alone. During those five days, I was sitting in the middle of the stream on a rock, and I was writing in my journal, and a butterfly landed on my knee, and something hit me; nature hit me, and I felt okay; for one of the first times in my life, I felt okay.

Regina Meredith: Safe and actually nurtured.

Elisabeth Hoekstra: Yes, I did. I didn't have any drugs or alcohol in me, so I felt good. And I remember, those five days alone were very healing for me, and I actually graduated, and I went home and had a lot of empathy and regret for how I treated my parents. I thought everything was going to be awesome, and I was on a new path at this point; I had a new mind frame.

And then, they hit me again with, "You're going to go to boarding school".

Chapter 6

Boarding School

Elisabeth Hoekstra: They only gave me a week at home with my friends and I had fallen in love with my boyfriend, so for the first time, we told each other we loved each other. I was looking forward to building a relationship, and my parents came back with, "Oh no, you're going to a boarding school in New Hampshire" and I lived in Michigan. I asked, "When do I leave?" Them, "In a couple of days, pack your bags". I didn't know what else to do, so I shrugged, "Okay, you want to do this to me?"

Regina Meredith: There was some abandonment going on.

Elisabeth Hoekstra: Oh, yeah. So, at that time, I thought, "I don't care", I shut down my emotions and felt nothing. I went and I completely dismissed all the growth I had gained from boot camp. I was back to rebel, complete rebel.

Regina Meredith: Yeah, because who do you have to answer to, when nobody loves you?

Elisabeth Hoekstra: That's exactly how I felt, just abandoned; I went to boarding school.

Regina Meredith: It sounds like that boot camp was actually a pretty wise thing for them to have you go to on certain levels.

Elisabeth Hoekstra: I think it was.

Regina Meredith: It was harsh and weird and all, and you did get nature.

Elisabeth Hoekstra: Yes. I was in nature; I felt good; I felt connected. I learned a lot about surviving in the woods. I have those tools in my back pocket now, and I feel I could survive anywhere.

Regina Meredith: Well, to feel like you're ready to honor your mom and dad, and then come back and find out they're not ready to deal with it again just yet, maybe you needed more distance.

Elisabeth Hoekstra: Yeah, it killed me. It brought me back to the feelings of when I was a child, and the emptiness; it always felt like my heart and stomach were going to sink through the ground, empty in here, and it would physically hurt. Now, when they told me I had to leave again, I stopped and sunk, "Ugh".

My protection mechanism to shut it all off kicked in; I completely shut emotion off, completely shut any type of empathy off. Told myself, "All right", and just mad.

Regina Meredith: So, that's set up now, if the sexual part set up your life until then, rejection setup what followed, were all these forces came together, and you were out of control.

Elisabeth Hoekstra: Oh, yeah, completely. It was bad.

Regina Meredith: Yeah, we have the setup there. Okay. So, you went to boarding school, and yoo-hoo, you partied even more; you don't owe anybody anything.

Elisabeth Hoekstra: Yep, and that's where I started pills.

Regina Meredith: And then, pills; drugs. So, really briefly, the boarding school essentially wanted to kick you out. So, you had a choice; your parents could come get you, or they could kick you out, and that goes on your record.

Elisabeth Hoekstra: Right. It was a three-strike rule. I had gotten in trouble for fighting, smoking cigarettes, and partying. And so, I had two strikes, I was about to get my third because my boyfriend had come visit me and they heard beer bottles clanking in his car, so they caught us, and before they could kick me out of school, my parents pulled me out.

Regina Meredith: So, after you returned home, things were a little more normal for a year or so.

Elisabeth Hoekstra: Oh, man, no.

Regina Meredith: So, you went back home to your parents, and no, it wasn't normal.

Elisabeth Hoekstra: No, not at all. Now I hated them. I wanted to be out of the house. I snuck out more. I was partying more. I was on drugs at the time because the boarding school experience introduced me to Adderall. I'm like, "This is great. I get to stay up forever, and I can do all my work", but even through all this craziness and the partying and everything, I still liked to be a good student.

Regina Meredith: Yeah, that's one of the really interesting parts of you; this super high function alongside the super low dysfunction.

Elisabeth Hoekstra: My friends would actually get mad at me because I would skip school so much and still get A's on everything.

Regina Meredith: An interesting and beautiful part of your nature, that you have these two sides and were able to live side by side for so many years.

Chapter 7

The King Pin

Regina Meredith: Okay, now, you're out of high school. You meet your ex-boyfriend, of course, he was a drug dealer because that would suit your lifestyle very well. It sounds like you were high all the time. This was in Michigan, you lived with your drug dealer boyfriend, and you would go downstairs, there would be drug dealers from Mexico, making deals in the mornings. Okay, now he gets busted. Sounds like he was psychotic. There was some other stuff that went on; so, let's talk about how that part wrapped up because we got a lot more of this to come.

Elisabeth Hockstra: Right, he was very abusive, and at the time, I hated myself, and I was on drugs and alcohol all the time. I lived in a dream state all the time; I didn't know what was going on. He kept me high, always had drugs available, and would push me to take them. But he was over-the-top verbally abusive and physically abusive. I remember trying to leave him at one point, and he told me if I ever left him he would throw acid all over me so no one would want me because I would be so ugly. I tried to leave again on Christmas, and he pistol whipped me; he held the pistol at my head and made me stay. Surprisingly, I remember thinking, "Oh he loves me".

Him saying these things and getting so upset while I was trying to leave, coupled with my past trauma, led me to believe this meant love, and I felt loved.

Regina Meredith: Because he didn't want you to go; he must love you.

Elisabeth Hoekstra: He must love me because he would go to the heights of throwing acid on me if I ever left him. Oh my gosh.

Regina Meredith: He'd risk going to prison to do these things to keep you.

Elisabeth Hoekstra: Yes, to keep me here. And oh my gosh, I can pull that type of emotion out of him where he would actually pistol whip me; he must really care. So, let me stay here and be supportive is how my mind worked at the time. But yeah, he was a major drug dealer, and one day, while he was gone doing a drop, helicopters appeared above my house, and I asked, "What's going on?" and my girlfriend, we had a friend staying with us, she says, "There are helicopters up here", and suddenly came a 'bang, bang, bang' at the door; it was a bunch of cops. I opened the door to huge guns in my face, wondering "What is happening here?" but at the time, I was still frozen; I didn't care. I'm thinking, "Okay, any type of authority figure, don't try me because I don't care what you're going to do". They said, "We got a search warrant," I challenged them, "No, you don't, show me the search warrant". I'm talking all my smack to these people with huge guns in my face.

Regina Meredith: You were hanging out in Detroit too.

Elisabeth Hoekstra: Yes, I was going back and forth between Detroit and Kalamazoo. I remember now my reaction towards the cops. I was so deeply frozen I didn't care about the fact I had guns in my face, I was fearless at that point, saying, "I don't care; shoot me, already. You're not coming into this house; shoot me". After they showed me the warrant, all I could say was, "Oh shit," and open the door for them. They came in, they searched the house, and come to find out the intrusion ended in the biggest drug bust in the history of Kalamazoo, Michigan at that time.

Regina Meredith: Wow. You were with a big-time dealer and didn't know, I guess.

Elisabeth Hoekstra: I knew something, but not to the extent of what was happening, not that I'd even care. And, yeah, these events are real choppy in my memory, too. We came back to the house, and I looked around and immediately broke down, broken-hearted. This brought me out of disassociation/freeze, and I felt the pain in my gut as I took what I was seeing in. It looked like a tornado hit the house. Everything was turned over, broken, ripped. I mean, pillows were cut, everything was everywhere. I felt the sinking feeling I get in my stomach when things go bad. I could only think, "This is my home, and my home is destroyed; this is the worst".

I left, and I didn't come back there. It was too traumatizing. I actually left all my stuff there, even my car; I didn't turn back. I visited my ex, the drug dealer, in jail and I found out that he was cheating on me with his baby's mother. I decided, "Screw this", his cheating was the last straw for me. I washed my hands with him and that house.

Regina Meredith: Like, everything you put out wasn't enough.

Elisabeth Hoekstra: Basically. I left and moved to Detroit.

Regina Meredith: And then, life got interesting.

Chapter 8

Exotic Asia

Regina Meredith: You decided we're going to go ahead, and why not use your body? It works for you. So, you became a stripper when they had heavy laws on no touching, a no-touch stripper, but you became excellent at it.

Elisabeth Hoekstra: Oh yeah. I was in high demand because I was the exotic Asian. All these strip clubs offered to pay me on top of working for tips. I was their main attraction, and for a while, I used my looks to make a lot of money. This career definitely instigated the heaviest drug use of my life.

Regina Meredith: Just to do the job; just to show up and do the job. What were you taking at that time?

Elisabeth Hoekstra: I was continuously drunk and taking a lot of ecstasy. I took a lot of Adderall to stay awake, and I don't think I was on cocaine yet; I think I tried it a couple of times, but I was heavily on ecstasy and Adderall.

Regina Meredith: And again, I point out, you're tiny. You're 4'11" now as a grown-up lady, and so, this little body. I'd have died the first day in the life you were living. I don't know how your body was able to withstand all the abuse.

Elisabeth Hoekstra: Oh yea, it's withstood so much. I would take 6,7,8 ecstasy pills in a night, mixed with alcohol, mixed with Adderall. I don't know how I survived.

Regina Meredith: You have this incredible intense force of will.

Elisabeth Hoekstra: Yeah, I think so.

Regina Meredith: Yeah. And if you're going to do something, you do it all the way.

Elisabeth Hoekstra: I go hard at any and everything I do, whether it be "negative" or "positive". If I'm going to be a stripper, I'm going to be the best damn stripper there ever has been. Haha

Regina Meredith: Which serves you well in life. As time goes on for you, it'll keep serving you well. But this time, you did that well too. So, after, you also said you started running a prostitution service.

Elisabeth Hoekstra: Yes. I met these girls, and they were already prostitutes, you know? So, I offered, "Hey, I can help promote you guys and get you more clients".

Regina Meredith: You're good at marketing.

Elisabeth Hoekstra: Oh, man, yes. I started by putting ads in back pages and made some good money. I became known by some of the guys in Detroit city as a "Madam" for a while. You know it was—

Regina Meredith: But you started doing a little bit of drug dealing at the time too?

Elisabeth Hoekstra: Well I had already been dealing drugs. I actually started dealing drugs when I was fourteen years old.

Regina Meredith: You now went to oxycontin and other things too.

Elisabeth Hoekstra: I actually only sold oxycontin in high school for a very short period of time because of the guy I was selling it to; my monetary return was amazing, so I was making a lot of money. But the guy's girlfriend had come to me, upset sharing, "Listen, you're ruining his life; he's not the same person. All he cares about is spending money for these drugs," and she begged me to stop.

I remember thinking, "Whoa, I don't want to ruin anybody's life", my intention was never to have a negative impact on anyone's life.

Regina Meredith: You just thought he needed a party like you did.

Elisabeth Hoekstra: Exactly. So, I completely stopped selling oxycontin.

Regina Meredith: Interesting. So, there, you had a real conscience, "That wasn't what I thought I was doing". What you thought you were doing was helping people feel numb like you.

Elisabeth Hoekstra: Yes, subconsciously I think. On the surface, I didn't see anything wrong when I was making a lot of money. People wanted to smoke weed and do drugs and have fake IDs, and I provided these things for my whole high school. And after I moved to Detroit, I hustled inside the strip clubs selling ecstasy pills. Selling drugs was a pretty consistent thing during my life.

Regina Meredith: So, now we go through this, you've been really popular, and you're getting some business for the girls and all. But also, you are discovered as like a little princess-sized model. Exotic Asian princess model.

Elisabeth Hoekstra: Interestingly enough, before I was even of age to be in Detroit's hottest clubs, I was able to get in with fake IDs and my looks. All of my girlfriends were pretty; they were gorgeous. Our beauty made it easy to get walked right up to VIP, pop bottles, and party with the best of them.

At eighteen, I walked out of one of the hottest clubs in Detroit at the time, and I got discovered by DJ Knice—a popular Detroit DJ, and he wanted me to present the Detroit Hip Hop Awards in 2006. I thought, "Oh wow, that's going to be fun".

Chapter 9

Asia Rain

Elisabeth Hoekstra: Everything shifted at that point; I put the prostitution stuff away with the girls. I tried to build a whole different thing for myself because I couldn't focus on too much at once. So yes, I developed into this model. Dj Knice gave me the name Asia Rain, and from there I "blew up" in Detroit. I was popular, and having photoshoots and—

Regina Meredith: How did you feel about all the attention when your own self-esteem was actually quite low on a deep level? How did all the attention make you feel?

Elisabeth Hoekstra: I was almost numb; I was still in kind of a dream state at this time. I liked the attention, but I expected it. I know I'm going to be the best at whatever I do, so it was nothing. It was more of, "I know", you know?

With my work ethic, I was at every single audition. I had photoshoots all night until the crack of dawn, literally, because I thought at the time,

"Okay, more pictures". I was working harder than ever, and yes, I liked the attention because it was familiar. I had kind of gotten attention for my looks since I was young.

Regina Meredith: So, it wasn't anything new; it was another iteration of it. Next, you packed your car, and you headed to LA. Classic story.

Elisabeth Hoekstra: Yes. I moved to LA. I drove out there with $300, my minivan, and a dream. I stayed in LA for about two years, and a whole bunch of stuff happened out there. I was homeless for a while. I lived on Venice Beach for a couple of weeks. I lived out of my van. I used to go to this internet café to send my pictures out for auditions. Remember internet cafés, hahaha. So, next to the internet café, there was a little hair shop owned by an Asian woman, and I remember when I was homeless, she would wash my hair and let me wash up in her place. She took to me because I was Asian.

Regina Meredith: Because she knew you were a little lost one at the time.

Elisabeth Hoekstra: Yes, exactly. So, I could still get ready for my shoots and stuff. I was homeless for about three weeks before I met a couple of people through auditions and stuff, and I started sleeping on couches from there.

Regina Meredith: Well then, you met a reality star.

Elisabeth Hoekstra: Well, almost. I met this gangster guy who had a huge crush on me, and he had a big house in Granada Hills. I lived there for a while, and yes, at an audition, I met a reality star, and he ended up moving into the house too, along with another reality star and his child.

It was like a dream. We had so much fun. I remember he would go to auditions—he was big-time then, so I would tag along and party at all these different huge events with all these different celebrities. By now, I was in major music videos. I was in magazines, I was popular, I was hosting parties. So, I was shaking hands with different celebrities on a regular basis. I dated a couple and ended up on red-carpets and huge events. Externally, I was living the life.

Regina Meredith: It seemed like you have it all together, but you didn't.

Elisabeth Hoekstra: No. I was on massive amounts of drugs, and I was always drunk. I had all this energy, and I didn't need to sleep. We would go to after-hours and party until six, seven in the morning, lay down for an hour, get back up, and start drinking again. Consistent alcohol use all the time.

Regina Meredith: And you could hold a lot of it.

Elisabeth Hoekstra: Oh yeah!

Regina Meredith: You said you and your girlfriend at one point were so poor, you'd have McDonald's $1 hamburgers by day to keep some food in you to be able to split a bottle of vodka.

Elisabeth Hoekstra: Oh, Grey Goose. We needed to have our Grey Goose, so we would spend all our money on Grey Goose. That was our thing. Even through the dysfunctional relationships, I always had someone around me, supporting me. A specific instance I will remember for the rest of my life. I was living in CA with, Veronica, who greatly helped me.

We met at the strip clubs in Detroit and rolled together for years. She offered to go strip and make money for the both of us so I could focus on my modeling career when we lived in LA. I'm not sure if I ever told her, but I needed her to do that at the time. I couldn't have grown to the level I was at without her support and belief in me. I will love her forever even though we've grown apart for various reasons, but that, I will never forget.

Regina Meredith: So, a burger and a half a fifth of vodka at night. And now, you finally reached California's drinking age, twenty-one. You have a lot of living under your belt.

Elisabeth Hoekstra: Oh yes, I was already deep into the party scene, but all of it is very spotty because I was always high and drunk.

Regina Meredith: You had a lot of blackout periods.

Elisabeth Hoekstra: Yes, and I started doing cocaine in Cali. It was huge and "normal" in Cali, so I think that's another reason I was able to go, go, go. It was normal to snort a line and go run the hills for the Hollywood girl. So, that was the whole gig, lots of different parties; it was just one big party for about two years straight in California for me.

Regina Meredith: So, what happened next, because it appears you went back to Detroit?

Elisabeth Hoekstra: I really don't know how I got there. Everything is such a blur.

Chapter 10

T.C. – My Best Friend

Regina Meredith: How did the California thing end? Why did you go back to Detroit?

Elisabeth Hoekstra: It was getting too expensive. I thought it was a little ridiculous to keep on trying to live that life. And oh, I actually had moved to Louisiana because they had movie credits at that time. An ex-boyfriend of mine moved me down there with him, and I was supposed to be in a major movie. And because they were providing incentives to shoot movies there, they were filming a lot of big stuff in Louisiana. I lived with him for a bit. We ended up getting into a massive argument over him cheating, and he took me out of the movie, which sucked.

Regina Meredith: So, you went back to Detroit.

Elisabeth Hoekstra: I lived in Louisiana probably for about a year before I moved back to Detroit. I learned stability by holding a regular job down there though. I worked at GNC.

Regina Meredith: You started learning about health and nutrition.

Elisabeth Hoekstra: Yes, and I loved it. It was everything for me. It provided stability, and I could nerd out on these vitamins. I actually became the best salesman in the region.

Regina Meredith: But it didn't stop what you did at night, did it?

Elisabeth Hoekstra: No, no, I was still drinking, no drugs at the time but heavy drinking. My boyfriend was never home; so, I started drinking alone.

Regina Meredith: You were trying to take care of yourself in new ways; the best you knew how, but it still wasn't hitting you that this numbing out at night was probably counterproductive to what you're learning by day.

Elisabeth Hoekstra: Right, exactly. And a lot of traumatic stuff happened while I was away in Louisiana. One of my friends died, my best friend Jenay's younger sister actually, she was one of my best friends also. She was only a year younger than us.

I moved back to Michigan shortly after my friend's funeral. Pretty soon after I moved back to Michigan, my closest friend, my very best friend, my brother—TC, the one I had met back when I was fourteen living at the apartment in Lansing, was murdered. That one broke me for a while. I was repeatedly going to funerals during that time too, and it was, "Ugh". [cries softly]

Regina Meredith: You were starting to kind of see some of the consequences; even though you weren't registering them, you were seeing the consequences of the really fast life you were living.

Elisabeth Hoekstra: Right. I actually was with TC the day before he was killed. I remember he was all excited about a new apartment. And at that time, I was trying to do something different with my life because I had the GNC thing; I didn't want to sell drugs anymore.

Regina Meredith: You sold vitamins, and you were good at it.

Elisabeth Hoekstra: Yes. TC and I had a conversation, and he said, "Oh, I'm about to go to this game tonight, and I'm about to sell these things, and I'm about to make all this money. Look at my place". He was all hype. I chided him, "Dude, you got this new place, just be cool". I left that day, and going back to my place he called me, and I didn't answer because I didn't want to deal with [cries], yeah, I mean, that was the night that he got shot and killed.

I woke up to 50,000 calls from all my friends, all his boys, and the news broke me. I thought I was still dreaming. I hardly ever felt emotion throughout my life because I was always numbing it, but that sinking feeling came back that day. I was uncontrollably crying. He was my best friend. We talked every single day. Before LA, I had lived with him for a while. Him and his mom. He helped me through a lot of stuff emotionally, and he [cries]—

Regina Meredith: What was his name?

Elisabeth Hoekstra: TC, Tyrone Childs. Rest in peace. We were so close.

Regina Meredith: He sounds like he was the one rock in your life.

Elisabeth Hoekstra: Yes, he was always there for me.

Regina Meredith: And he wasn't the boyfriend, and he wasn't a classic gangster. He was just your friend.

Elisabeth Hoekstra: Correct. He was funny, a comedian. He would do comedy shows, and he would also rap. He wasn't hard like gangster hard, but he knew how to freestyle better than anyone I have ever met. He was the comic relief in my life.

Regina Meredith: He was a real friend.

Elisabeth Hoekstra: Yes, he helped me. He was always there. He helped my modeling Asia Rain career. After I stopped dancing, I would do these dance contests. I knew I would win because he would bring all his friends and they would cheer the loudest for me, and I would win because the contest was determined by the amount of noise the crowd made. He did stuff like that all the time.

Regina Meredith: Yeah, that would be devastating when he was your rock and your funny guy. So, that's over.

Elisabeth Hoekstra: That was a rough one.

Chapter 11

Bonnie and Clyde

Regina Meredith: At this time, you probably thought it might be nice if your life could go in a better direction, but instead, you met a guy that you thought was one of the most beautiful men you'd ever seen.

Elisabeth Hoekstra: Yeah, that was crazy. Coming from TC's funeral, I remember I was with my girlfriend, Veronica. We were driving going to our friend's house. We pull up, and I see this guy coming out of the house, and I'm, WOW. He was all jacked, super muscular, and I'm, "Who is this guy?". I asked my girlfriend who he was, and she said, "Oh, that's B; he just got out". And I asked, "Oh, introduce me".

Regina Meredith: Of course. He just got out of prison; that's a decent portfolio for you.

Elisabeth Hoekstra: Yep, I was thought, "Oh, perfect guy here, just out, all muscular", okay.

Regina Meredith: Had a lot of time to work out.

Elisabeth Hoekstra: Oh yeah. We met, and the attraction was immediate, we matched very well, and about two weeks later, we moved in together. We became the modern-day Bonnie and Clyde.

Regina Meredith: You guys were on a rampage. Credit card fraud, drug dealing, lots of parties, and hustling. You said you were making, on the credit card hustle alone, $6,000 to $8,000 a day.

Elisabeth Hoekstra: Yeah, at one point, I considered, "We should stop because I think this is getting too good, we will get caught soon". I knew how the game worked.

Regina Meredith: What else was he up to? I mean, he'd been in prison for something. So, what was his game?

Elisabeth Hoekstra: He was the mastermind of a bank robbery when he was a teenager, so he got sent away. We met young; we met when he was twenty-two, I think I was twenty-three. And so, he was still hustling, but he was hustling weed, and at that time, it was super illegal. Credit cards and ecstasy pills were my hustle, so we were both making crazy amounts of money. We would spend $5-10 grand in strip clubs every night throwing it on the girls, partying and popping bottles. We were both heavy on drugs, too, because of the connections I had; we always kept more than a hundred pills in the house. We were living the "good life".

Regina Meredith: Oh my God. The people benefiting the most were the girls in the club because you knew their situation, and you tipped nicely.

Elisabeth Hoekstra: Oh man. They got all our money. It was a rampage for a while.

Regina Meredith: Yeah, I guess you had empathy for them, having been there.

Elisabeth Hoekstra: I was partying; I loved it. We went on a rampage doing Bonnie & Clyde stuff and being on drugs, and that was probably the most drugs I've ever been on in my life. And, yeah, I remember wanting a change, telling my guy, "Listen, let's just gather as much money as we can, let's move".

We were planning to move to Atlanta within a week. Well, that didn't happen because we got caught.

I remember this like it was yesterday. Me and him were at a Best Buy hustling, and at that time, I was too confident. I was fearless. The person at the cash register was trying to hold us up. B, was like, "Let's go, let's go". I'm, "Pfffff, we're good; stop it, it's going to be fine". He could see that something wasn't right. The cashier was trying to hold us up because the cops were coming. As soon as we walked outside, the scene played like the movies. Twenty cop cars pulled up on us. I thought to myself, "Oh shit, we're in trouble". And I remember laughing, thinking this is not good, sooooo not good!

Regina Meredith: Did it not hit you at that time? Because you had that whole Bonnie & Clyde kind of irreverence for everyone and all of life, and you simply didn't care. It didn't occur to you that you might end up in the slammer.

Elisabeth Hoekstra: Right. No, not at all. Who laughs at the fact that a million cops pull up to arrest us for doing a bunch of illegal stuff? Well, I did. My fear center in my brain was completely shut down during a lot of my life. I look back on these things and wonder what the hell was I thinking.

Regina Meredith: Because you've gotten by with everything so far.

Elisabeth Hoekstra: Pretty much. I always thought everything was cool. The day we got caught was a Friday, on a hot summer day. They ran towards him first and held him up. They literally ran right past me. One even said to me as he ran past, "You need to watch who you hang with", and they held him up.

I'm thinking, "Huh? Little do you know this is my hustle we're getting caught for right now…". Racism at its finest, terrible. So, they searched the car, found the credit cards, cuffed us, and stuck us in the back of the cop car. We could have died that day; it was probably about 95 °F outside, and they had us in the back of a car with the windows up, and it was getting hotter and hotter and hotter, I could hardly breathe. The way these cops treat people is extremely inhumane. I don't care what a person does; criminal or not, humans should be treated with respect. You're supposed to be innocent until proven guilty. The system is backward in that way. You're definitely treated as if you're guilty until proven innocent.

Regina Meredith: Probably a hot summer; by that time, in the cop car, it was a hundred degrees.

Elisabeth Hoekstra: It was bad. They were doing a thorough search, so it was taking forever. As they were searching my car, B and I were in the back of the cop car for hours. I remember talking to him, still confident and unphased. "Don't worry, we'll have to stay a couple of days, but we'll be out by Monday. We can't get arraigned; it's the weekend, we'll get arraigned on Monday, and then, we'll be out, and we'll be good".

Chapter 12

Locked Up

Regina Meredith: So, you knew the system?

Elisabeth Hoekstra: Yes. I had been to jail a couple of times prior to all of this, not for extended stays, and not for anything serious so I wasn't completely blind to what was going to happen.

They took us to jail, and they stuck us in holding where they stick the drunk people to sober up. The tank had glass so we could see everything that was happening. I remember seeing a guy in a suit who looked out of place. He walked by, and when I saw him again, B was following him.

I mouthed to him, "What's going on?" as he followed the guy to this private office. Some time passed and they both walked by again. B mouth to me, "Don't say anything", I know better thinking, "Duh, but okay".

I got taken out, and to my surprise, it was the Secret Service. The Secret Service gets involved whenever it's a credit card issue. He started trying to intimidate and threaten me with all these years in prison, my response was, "Screw you," "Yeah, you don't know anything; you don't know shit". My attitude was, "I don't give a fuck, do something".

Regina Meredith: Well, you're a little gangster, yourself.

Elisabeth Hoekstra: Hah, well, I was in deep freeze, completely disassociated, so nothing scared me. This really didn't scare me at all. I had zero fear around this event up to this point. "Do something. Lock me up then," I told him. I thought, still, we were good. I will deal with being uncomfortable a couple of days until we get arraigned and get out.

They ended up sticking me in max because I had never been to that jail before, and they didn't know how to classify me. There was a mid, medium, and max area of the jail. They put me in max to observe me and figure out my classification. I was in max for a long time, way longer than the average person, I think because of the seriousness of my charges and because they had no idea who I was. Being in max was awful. It was a tiny little cement box. They gave us these tiny skinny pads to sit and sleep on that weren't even pads; they were disgusting, dirty, broken, and ripped. I was not allowed to have anything because it was "max," so it was me, the broken pad, and the cement walls, for days. I remember going a little crazy from being alone so much. At times, they would throw other women in with me, but they were in and out quickly. So, I would have days where—

Regina Meredith: Plus, you had no drugs. So, your body was trying to detox fast.

Elisabeth Hoekstra: Yeah, no drugs. I thought to myself, "When am I going to get out of here? This is weird. I thought I'd be out by now". I started playing chess on the ground with my imagination. I created pieces with bible paper and tried to scratch an actual chess board on the ground. I didn't have anything to write with, so I used my imagination. I was losing my mind, to be honest. I was in max for about two weeks which is a seriously long time to be without human interaction. The interaction I was getting was super sparse.

Regina Meredith: Where did you learn to play chess along the way?

Elisabeth Hoekstra: I love chess! I was actually in the chess club when I was younger.

Regina Meredith: Well, of course, when you were seven. Yes, okay, let's continue.

Elisabeth Hoekstra: Haha. So yeah, the weekend that I thought we would be locked up turned into months. The worst feeling is not knowing when you're going to get out, when you'll be free again. Every time you go to court, you think you're going to get out, so hopes would go up then get repeatedly crushed. This jail was also, by far, the worst in Michigan. They actually had lawsuits against them for unfair treatment of inmates. County jails are always known to be worse than prisons. This is how broken the system is—they treat you like animals. I had my period, and I bled through my pants. I remember begging the CO to give me a new pair of pants, and she wouldn't. She just laughed and ignored me. So, I sat with dirty pants for days. It was so embarrassing; I didn't even get off my bunk.

That's the type of treatment that you get when you're in there; they literally treat you like the scum of the earth. They don't treat you like you're a human. We had one out of the multiple CO's that was actually nice to us. ONE, out of all of them. They treated us like shit continuously for no reason, other than the fact we were "criminals". But you know, innocent until proven guilty, right?

Even the food that they gave us was expired. Every single day we ate a piece of bologna and two pieces of white bread with expired milk; every single day for dinner. We didn't get let outside; I didn't see the sun not one time while I was there. Not one time. That alone is abuse. I understand that breaking the law is wrong and understand that I should have been in trouble. I had to experience this consequence for sure. BUT that does not make it okay for others to treat you like an animal no matter the situation, at least in my opinion. Jail and prisons are supposed to rehabilitate people, punish, yet positively change them. These places do the opposite of that.

Regina Meredith: So, this was literally your low point.

Elisabeth Hoekstra: Yeah, it was pretty low, but I made the best out of it, though. I started doing workout classes and stuff in my pod.

Regina Meredith: Yeah, sure you would have. So, you were working out, and you created classes for your roomies.

Elisabeth Hoekstra: Yes, I was pretty popular in there. All the girls loved me because I was high in energy, and I tried to make the best out of the depressing situation we were all in. I tried to turn jail into a camp in my head because it was pretty depressing, especially coming from the fast life B and I lived. I remember I would pay some of the girls in the commissary to let me take their depression meds so that I could sleep. I was trying to self-soothe while I was in there with any drug I could get my hands on.

Regina Meredith: Right. You were doing the hustle.

Elisabeth Hoekstra: Yes. I was definitely taking a bunch of depression meds in there, so I was a bit spacey. But yeah, I remember when I finally got out, the whole pod of girls, there were probably about thirty of them, was all clapping; some were crying. The CO that left me in bloody pants was the one who walked me out. She looked at me and said, "Oh, look at you, Miss Popular, they don't want you to leave, but I know you'll be back." I laughed my way out of there. I knew at this point I would NOT be back.

I got out before B. The reason why we didn't get out for so long was that they put a quarter-million-dollar cash-only bond on us. They did that because we got caught far away from where we lived so we were a flight risk, and because of the seriousness of the charges. When we got to circuit court under a new judge, he put a cash surety on the bond, so my mom actually put up her house for me. And that's how I was able to get out.

Regina Meredith: That was an amazing gesture on her part.

Elisabeth Hoekstra: Oh yeah. My mom, through all the crazy, never turned her back on me; not ever, not ever. I love her so much for that. I would not be who I am today at all if she wasn't the #1 rock in my life.

Regina Meredith: Even if you thought she turned her back on you when they wanted to send you to boarding school.

Elisabeth Hoekstra: Yeah, I know now, being mature, I know that they were all only doing what they thought—

Regina Meredith: Doing the best they knew how. Absolutely. So, that's an incredible gesture on her part to have done that for you.

Chapter 13

Put in Cuffs – The Heartbreaking Moment

Regina Meredith: So, you're out, where's he? And at what point does the baby start?

Elisabeth Hoekstra: He was still locked up. Now, I go back to our home in metro Detroit. Coming back to our house was so traumatizing for me. Entering the house, I had another stomach and heart-sinking moment because my home was a complete wreck. Cops had raided it. Furniture was ripped, clothes were thrown everywhere, there were holes in the walls, everything was in disarray. They took all my jewelry, my nice clothes, things were strewn everywhere, and everything was broken. This is now the second time this had happened in my life. When you go back, and you see your home destroyed, I can't even explain the feeling; it's heartbreaking. [softly cries]

Regina Meredith: Oh, I can't imagine. There's nowhere to return. So, when did you see B again?

Elisabeth Hoekstra: He ended up getting out a couple of months later when the judge put a 10% bond on him. As soon as the judge assigned the amount, I worked hard to get cash so we could put the 10% down and he could get out. When he got out, we come to find out he had caught a separate fed case for weed. And so, they were after him; they were looking for him while he was in County. And so, we went on the run. He didn't want to turn himself in to the feds.

So, we were hiding in Lansing, and I remember the exact day I got pregnant. It was around New Year's, and we were so high off of ecstasy. Something was different though, I felt it. I knew I was going to be pregnant. I didn't say anything to him, but I knew. A couple of weeks later, I took the test and found out I was pregnant. We discussed it, and I told him, "Look, I can't get rid of the baby, and I got to go through with this." He's behind me, "Okay, all right. So, what do we got to do? How are we gonna do this?".

My life shifted. I stopped smoking cigarettes, and I stopped doing drugs. I didn't want to hurt the baby. I would have a glass of wine here and there but—

Regina Meredith: You were pretty clean.

Elisabeth Hoekstra: Yes

Regina Meredith: So, you did understand the seriousness about being responsible for another being, other than yourself, for the little being you were growing. Didn't B end up having to go back to prison?

Elisabeth Hoekstra: Yes, he was on house arrest the whole time I was pregnant; it was very stressful. My Pregnancy was stressful because, for a while, I had to work for the both of us to pay our bills, all while going back and forth to court. B was stuck at home and depressed; he went into a deep depression. I mean, who wouldn't be? On house arrest and going through this again, facing prison time, again, this time with a new baby on the way. He was in a whole different place mentally, and it was hard on our relationship.

It was difficult, but I remember going to court, and because I was pregnant, the prosecutor felt bad for us. The prosecutor said, "Okay, well, you can have a couple of months to meet your baby until you have to turn yourself in". They gave us three or four months with the baby before he had to turn himself in. And yeah, the whole departure, it was [softly cries], it was heartbreaking. That was one of the hardest moments of my life. He had to turn himself in out of state. When it was time, we took a road trip to the city where the prison was and stayed at a hotel. We spent the night with baby Gabriel, he was only about four months at the time.

Regina Meredith: Beautiful boy.

Elisabeth Hoekstra: Yeah, oh man, he's my everything. And yes, I remember it's one of the most heartbreaking moments of my entire life—having to stroll my newborn baby into the prison and watch the guards take his father away in cuffs. Him saying goodbye to his baby, it was really hard. It was heartbreaking for him, especially; I can't imagine how he felt. But he's deep freeze, like me, so not too much emotion was present to be seen. That was rough. He kissed Gabe goodbye.

Regina Meredith: When did he see him again?

Elisabeth Hoekstra: We went and saw him once when he was in prison, but B didn't really want to see Gabriel while he was there. So, yeah, B didn't see him again until Gabe was about three. The drive there was strenuous, too, and with a new human, it was difficult to make the trip. After about a year of him being gone, I was changing, and so was our relationship. We ended up breaking up when he got home for various reasons.

Regina Meredith: Right. That was too hard for everybody.

Elisabeth Hoekstra: Yeah.

Regina Meredith: Well, it just keeps getting more interesting, that was sad, and that's tragic, breaking up and everything about it. But you don't stay down for very long.

Elisabeth Hoekstra: No, no. I just knew what I needed to do for Gabriel. So, at the time, I know I can't risk going to jail anymore because if I go to jail, who's going to watch the baby? So, I got on a more straight and narrow path.

Chapter 14

Assistant to the Master

Elisabeth Hoekstra: I started working a lot, trying to save money. I was working as a bartender and waitress at strip clubs because you make a ton of money. I signed up for school because I loved to cook. I thought maybe I should try something different. So, I was going to school to get a degree, working multiple jobs, and I was trying to support a newborn baby by myself. I was so busy for a long time.

I remember working all the time; I hardly saw my son because I was so busy trying to make the money to support him, all while going to school. So, he was always in daycares and with babysitters. At one point, I was taking a baking class, and with baking, you have to start very early. I remember I'd be working at the strip club until close, get out at 3:30 a.m. Sometimes, I would go straight to the gym and work out, and then go straight to class after the gym at 5:30 a.m. Sometimes, if it was too late, I would go in the parking lot of the school and sleep until I had to start class.

Regina Meredith: Are you doing any drugs at this point to be able to live through this lack of sleep?

Elisabeth Hoekstra: Yeah, I was doing Adderall to stay up and drinking in the evening at the strip clubs.

Regina Meredith: Okay, so, that continued; you could stay up long enough to do your schedule.

Elisabeth Hoekstra: Yeah, and it was still hard for me to work in strip clubs because I could sense the dysfunction, and I didn't like it. People would buy me drinks all the time, so I was drunk all the time.

Regina Meredith: Adderall to keep you awake to do your job, go to school and everything, apprenticing and all that.

Elisabeth Hoekstra: Yep, I became an assistant, well, I was the sous chef to the master pastry chef there, and I became phenomenal at pastry. You don't actually apply to be a sous chef, you get chosen to be a sous chef, and I was one of the chosen. So, I was very talented at pastries; I picked it up fast and ended up getting a 4.0 in all of my pastry classes and was on the Dean's list.

Regina Meredith: I admire you. I love baking, but I don't have your skill; that's amazing what you did. I've seen pictures of what you've created; you're the real deal.

Elisabeth Hoekstra: Thank you, I loved it. The work was pretty, detailed, and dainty. I loved creating awesome-looking stuff. I was definitely trained by the right person. At that time, there were only six master pastry chefs in the U.S.A., and I was training under one of them. This led to my next job. I got picked up by one of the most prestigious country clubs in the country, Oakland Hills. The executive chef of the club told me to come interview. Come to find out later down the line he thought I was pretty, so he gave me a job, which was annoying.

Regina Meredith: Right. That's always part of the package.

Elisabeth Hoekstra: So annoying to me.

Regina Meredith: Yeah, instead of doing it on your actual skill, but you did have skill.

Elisabeth Hoekstra: Oh yeah, being pretty got me the job, but my talent in pastry kept my job.

Regina Meredith: And favoritism happens with pretty women in every line of work, it always has, throughout history, so, I wouldn't feel bad because you pulled it off. So, this was the beginning of starting to find function on a societal level that wasn't kind of, in the night or underground. This was a big deal.

Elisabeth Hoekstra: Yes. I was too busy to party. The only partying I did was working at the strip club, which was a party in itself. I wasn't partying outside of the job. I was incredibly focused at the time. I wanted my degree. I wanted to make good money and show my son some stability and structure. So yeah, it changed from there.

Regina Meredith: Yeah, and we're going to pick this story up with how those changes started showing themselves because you did some awesome things, which we're going to take a little break and we'll come back, and we'll do the second part of your story. The first one is kind of a life in pain and the fall; and the second one is the building back up with the same incredible force of will, which is amazing.

Chapter 15

Superwoman

Regina Meredith: So, you had been hired as an assistant pastry chef by a really prestigious country club, for a variety of reasons, then went on to open a top-notch restaurant as the pastry chef. That was just the start, but with your level of energy that wasn't the end of it. And let's talk about your whole foray. You met a man around this time, right? Again, a pretty woman met a man; he got you into real estate and flipping houses. Let's talk about that chapter in your life.

Elisabeth Hoekstra: At that time, I had been single for a while, so my girlfriends took it upon themselves to sign me up for Match.com. I'm thinking, "This is absolutely retarded", but I did it. I'm always open to try new things. So, the first date I went on was the last date I went on. I met this guy, D, and we hit it off. We ended up being together for a long time, four years to be exact. He was a real estate investor. At the time, he already owned a 15-unit multi in the richest part of Michigan, along with a couple of other multi-family homes in the area. And me, being co-dependent, from having zero self-love and being so frozen and trying to make everybody happy, I became very, very co-dependent to him right away.

I would be working at the country club, and I would be working 8, 10, 12 hour shifts. Then, right after work, I would go, and I would help D do his work, which was renovating every unit he owned.

So, we were gutting these apartments, which would involve ripping down walls, doing major dirty grunt work, hard labor. He taught me how to do plumbing and electric. I know how to lay tiles and do grout, and I learned a lot of stuff. I painted every single one of his properties; I was great at painting because I'm meticulous, with no mistakes. D had me carrying refrigerators, stoves, dishwashers, everything up multiple flights of stairs. He would yell at me if I would lose my grip; mind you, I'm just under 5' tall. I'm really strong, but I'm still tiny. I would literally help him carry refrigerators up multiple flights of stairs. It was a lot on me, and the yelling I continuously endured was awful.

Regina Meredith: Come on, now, people are going to say, "Who is this? Is this superwoman or what?"

Elisabeth Hoekstra: I was in gymnastics for thirteen years. I was strong, surprisingly strong. This set me up for the rest of my life. At the time I was with D, I worked out a lot. I've always been energetic and strong from the gymnastics training. Do you remember those old radiators, those cast-iron radiators? So, we carried a bunch of those out of buildings. Those things were hundreds of pounds. I remember I helped him take a washing machine off the back of his truck one day, and something had slipped. Then his hand slipped, and he cut his finger. Not as bad as what I was used to seeing in restaurants, but he had a super fear of blood, didn't do well with injuries.

I remember it like yesterday how he started screaming at me—he was a narcissist and the true definition of that exact word. He started screaming at me, blaming me, "How could you do that to me?!?!? Why would you do that!?!? Are you retarded?!". He was completely freaking out because of the little cut on his finger. He stayed mad at me for a while about that one. I mean, I was doing some hard labor at the time for him. But one good thing I took away from that horrible relationship was that I learned a lot.

Regina Meredith: Did you end up going and getting your real estate license?

Elisabeth Hoekstra: Yes. I got my real estate license because he told me I couldn't do it that I wouldn't be able to.

Regina Meredith: So, of course, you're going to do it on a dare.

Elisabeth Hoekstra: Yeah, exactly. I'm considering, "Oh, you're going to tell me I can't? I will show you I can". This has been the norm in my life. Tell me I can't do something, and watch me show you how I can. I got my real estate license, and I passed the exam on my first try, which is super rare because Michigan's real estate test to get your license is extremely hard. It's a whole different language; 90% of people who take it don't pass the first time. Afterward, I had to jump through some hoops because of my history of getting in trouble with the law; it was definitely difficult for me to get my license. But I took that challenge on. I was determined. I had multiple professionals write letters for me, including a church pastor, the master pastry chef I trained under, the executive chef at Oakland Hills Country Club, and a couple of others. Even throughout my crazy, I still held good relationships.

People believed in me because they saw the shiny part of me all the time. I was good at everything I tried, worked my ass off and became the best at everything I took on, and was fun and pleasant with everyone for the most part. I hid the dysfunction of unhappiness, drugs, and the trauma that was building underneath the surface. So, people were always supportive of me. I ended up getting my license, and that's where my next chapter started. I started real estate, but I also was still a chef, and I was trying to balance—

Regina Meredith: You were also a mother.

Elisabeth Hoekstra: Yes. So, I'm balancing a narcissist, a baby, being a chef, real estate, and it got to be too much. I had quit the bartending gig at the strip club when I became the pastry chef at the restaurant. There wasn't enough time in the day. Shortly after I got my real estate license, I ended up quitting the culinary industry, which is an extremely abusive industry.

Regina Meredith: Yeah, it's a tough life.

Elisabeth Hoekstra: Oh, man, I hardly saw my son which was awful. I was working twelve-sixteen hours by the time I became the pastry chef of this restaurant. I was their only pastry chef, so I would have to prepare thousands of desserts. It got to be overly repetitive.

I remember I was cleaning up pigs' blood off the floor of the restaurant one night at three in the morning on a Saturday, which was our deep cleaning night, so we'd be there until three, sometimes 4 a.m. cleaning. By that time, I started becoming conscious. "I hate this. This is awful. This is not who I am. I don't clean pig's blood off the ground. Like, what is this?" After the pig blood instance, I told myself, I'm going to stop, I'm going to quit. And it took a lot to drive me to that point because culinary was kind of something that I felt was my stability, and my structure was tied to.

It took a massive amount of confidence to leave. I didn't like it throughout the whole thing; it was hard labor. I liked making new desserts and seeing the beautiful creations come from my head to form AND taste good. The industry is what I hated. They work you until you die inside, literally. I mean, I hardly saw my son. I was so busy.

So, I ended up getting the guts and finally quitting, which was probably one of the greatest things I did in my life because it opened my world up to my true passion—business and entrepreneurship.

Regina Meredith: Yeah, and you were good. You ended up doing well in real estate, and I love what happened—you got some of the girls together. Let's talk about that. I love this.

Chapter 16

Outward Success But a Secret Addiction

Elisabeth Hoekstra: Yes! I got my real estate license and started doing well pretty quickly. I knew a lot of very wealthy people from working at the country club, so I was getting clients left and right. The deals were rolling in, so I figured, "Hmm, what would it be like to start a team?" I always liked to be different; throughout my whole life, I have always liked to stand out. I'm definitely not the crowd follower; I'm the trendsetter. There was planning involved in my head before I spoke the idea aloud. I thought, "What would make my team stand out?".

The idea came to me, straight download from the universe, "The pretty girl real estate team". So, I started recruiting exceptionally beautiful women and some of those women were previously strippers. I went to the strip clubs, and I talked to these girls. I recruited a couple of them, trained them, and mentored them. A few weeks after the idea came to me, I had a good amount of girls.

Regina Meredith: You had about thirty.

Elisabeth Hoekstra: At one time, I had a ton of agents. We were doing photo shoots; it was a lot of fun, and it was going well for a while. But there was a virus inside of my team. You have to keep a close eye on your business and keep your organization tight because if one bad apple comes in, it can ruin everything, and that's what happened to me. She ended up spreading lies about me and stealing some of my girls, bringing them with her to another brokerage.

From there, I considered, "Okay, take the girls, take some of the people". I still had ones that were loyal to me.

After that, I started recruiting men to be agents; the pretty girl team was dead. I lost a bit of interest after that drama happened within my team, and I started working more with my business partner at the time, helping him build his company. I helped take his company up 400% within a couple of years.

Regina Meredith: Doing what? In what function?

Elisabeth Hoekstra: He had an inspection company. This was also when I started diving a bit into politics and found out about terrible situations going on in Detroit City that were being swept under the rug.

Regina Meredith: It sounds like you have a real genius, a natural genius for marketing for one thing. You know how to put something in front of people so that it's appealing and they want to engage. Which is an amazing skill in this day and age.

Elisabeth Hoekstra: Right. Yes, and you know what? I was getting my brain back. I truly believe in neuroplasticity. And so, by me reading all the time and then thoroughly studying real estate, I like to be the best at everything I do, I solidified my commitment.

I was doing fewer drugs and I didn't have time to drink either. I felt I was getting my brain back a bit. Although, I was still in this awful relationship with the narcissist.

I wasn't on drugs every day, but I was on drugs and alcohol every three days or every four days only when I'd spend the night with him. I was miserable with him so I had to stay high to even act pleasant around him. I also fooled myself to believe I wasn't addicted because I was using every couple of days, not every day.

Regina Meredith: But you were hiding it from people, still?

Elisabeth Hoekstra: I was, and that's when I knew it was bad because I was hiding it from my best friends and family. D, the narcissist, didn't even know the entire time I'd be with him I was high and drunk. I could be functional on these drugs and alcohol, convincingly functional.

Regina Meredith: You had been your whole life.

Elisabeth Hoekstra: I was telling myself all these lies about my "non-addiction" throughout all this time, but yet still thriving out here with these businesses. I kind of hit a wall at one point. I was starting to see the dysfunction within my own life. I was a functional drug addict during that time. And I started getting more conscious and admitting it to myself because before I was hiding it even from my own conscious mind. I had never hidden my drugs or alcohol in the past.

Regina Meredith: Yeah, you were out there, partying. Let me ask you a question amidst this because it wasn't helpful. As you said, you were with your partner, who's a narcissist. And when you're with a narcissist, when anything goes down, it's your fault.

Elisabeth Hoekstra: Oh, everything, and I mean, everything.

Regina Meredith: And because some of the people watching this have struggled with narcissistic relationships, and so, what are a couple of the signs, steady hallmarks you noticed when you were in this, besides the fact that the blame all goes on you?

Elisabeth Hoekstra: I was always walking on eggshells. I didn't know what to say ever. It would take me instead of one second to think about what I was going to say; it would take me five, ten minutes because I was so afraid that I was going to get yelled at for saying the wrong thing. The yelling made me feel I was so ugly and like I was a piece of trash. Nothing I did was ever good enough. Every time I'd get ready to leave, he would show the man I fell in love with —his mask, which would reel me right back in. I lost a ton of my self-esteem in that relationship.

Regina Meredith: Even though you were greatly prospering during the day and in your endeavors, it's dangerous to be with a narcissist.

Elisabeth Hoekstra: Oh, yeah. He had me believing that I was the bottom of the earth, that I was stupid, and for those reasons, I had to prove to myself; I say, "Okay, I got a real estate license because he said I couldn't do it". But I had to prove to myself that I wasn't stupid because I started to believe that I was. He was never physically abusive, but throughout the abusive relationships I had experienced, I've got to say, this type of abuse—emotional abuse—was by far the worst.

Regina Meredith: Because he was messing with your head and sense of self.

Elisabeth Hoekstra: Yes. I completely lost my sense of self. Completely.

Regina Meredith: Well, the good thing is you guys ultimately broke up.

Elisabeth Hoekstra: Oh yes, thank God.

Chapter 17

Not My Style

E **lisabeth Hoekstra:** It's a funny story. I stayed with him longer because I thought he would never cheat on me. He was mean to me, he was an asshole, but I thought, "Okay, he's loyal. At least he's loyal", I had such low self-esteem. And come to find out at 2 a.m. one day, this girl knocks on the door and comes rushing in and comes running upstairs. "Oh, I recognize you; he said you were gay". I told her, "You stay, I'm leaving". After, the whole thing blew up.

He pushed her to the side and really begged for me back. He made her leave that night and told her he was in love with me. He said it was nothing with her, so I tried to work it out with him. I tried because I thought I was in love with him. But I couldn't. I couldn't be with him anymore. His narcissistic tendencies were peaking even through his fake apologies. This drama actually threw me into, a major depression. I didn't get out of bed for weeks.

Something happened, though, within those couple weeks, something amazing. I was watching a Tony Robbin's special on Netflix, and something he said deeply resonated with me, something he said to this girl he was talking to out in the crowd. He asked this girl,

"Who did you look up to more, and who did you want to be like more when you were growing up, your mom or your dad?" And, I don't know, something about his sentence clicked in my head. "Who did I look up to?". And with one sentence, that quick, I realized I was not my thoughts. I started disconnecting from my thoughts instead of thinking the voice in my head was me for once, for the first time in my life. And I realized, "Wow, I don't have to think negatively. I don't have to be depressed. I can change my thought process, and I don't have to be lying in bed and be upset about this guy. I can start to change the way I'm thinking".

From that day, I started working diligently on my thought process, trying to change the way I formulate thoughts. If I caught myself thinking anything negative, I would notice the thought and switch to a more positive one.

Regina Meredith: Which was the beginning of your journey back to what you are today, having overcome quite a bit. But along the way, you met a politician. You're in Michigan, still. So, you met a politician, and you started getting involved in politics. Because I mean, I really see very bright things for your future. You're a powerful person; you're going to do amazing things as you go through life. So, let's talk about this bit because I thought it was significant.

Elisabeth Hoekstra: Yes. I was so good at real estate, I got hired to be the exclusive agent. I went on to secure the most campaign offices in the shortest amount of time in campaign history for them. I broke records, and everybody loved me, of course. Haha. I had all my agents out getting campaign offices. It was work; it was a lot of work. It was literal, nonstop work, but I was thriving - I loved it. I really do well with chaos. I thrive in fast-paced atmospheres. I was super busy, and I remember I was at the Michigan's Governor birthday party, and I met a politician.

He was a State Senator, the minority leader of the Democratic party. I resonated with him because he recently had a kidney transplant, which my brother had gone through many years prior, and is currently looking for another kidney; my mother actually gave him

The Recipe to Elevated Consciousness

her kidney when he was sixteen. Transplants don't last forever. I understood what it was like.

We started dating, and when we dated, he started filling me in about all of these things going on in Detroit. He was the state Senator over part of Detroit city. And he started telling me the water is full of lead and all these terrible things. Everyone heard about Flint's water issue and how the high amounts of lead in the water there were poisoning the residents, but what they don't tell you is Detroit has the same issue. It's swept under the rug.

Regina Meredith: It's similar—

Elisabeth Hoekstra: It's bad, it's almost worse. These kids go to school with asbestos, lead-based paints, and toxic lights. And we look at Detroit, and we wonder why these kids aren't graduating, why they're dropping out, why the crime is higher...

Regina Meredith: Why they're not thriving.

Elisabeth Hoekstra: They're full of neurotoxins, that's why (among other things), and they're going to school and getting poisoned, and they're going home and getting poisoned. All Detroit's infrastructure is super old. Lead-based paint is rampant in Detroit city, asbestos is rampant, and bad water, you know? You start in a toxic environment, probably with a toxic family, and you go to another toxic environment, school or daycare. These kids have no chance from the start.

Regina Meredith: So, now, what are you doing with this?

Elisabeth Hoekstra: So, anytime I, PS: I don't watch the news; I don't watch disaster things, because if I see something bad and unnecessary, I feel I must change it. So, I was dating the State Senator and we started working on change together; strenuously, trying to change these things and trying to blow the whistle basically on what was going on in Detroit.

We were meeting in Lansing regularly, trying to change laws within Detroit City, so we could stop these kids from getting poisoned. I had the idea of demolishing the old schools and get funding so we could rebuild them. I had a connection to the Vietnam

Veterans of America and utilized that—he was Vice President of the national organization and was on board to help with this project. I was meeting with a lot of people trying to change this. And it was disheartening because a couple of meetings with some lobbyists and politicians didn't go well. The people we met with said it's going to take a lot of time to present something like this. "Come back in five years".

Regina Meredith: That's not your style.

Elisabeth Hoekstra: No. "Okay, not okay". This can't happen. It was very disheartening. Unfortunately, the State Senator I had been dating passed from Covid in 2020. RIP, Senator Hood III. He was a politician who truly cared for the people he served. His goals were never selfish. He truly loved his constituents.

Regina Meredith: So, this notion of, kind of, social activism is in you on a large scale.

Elisabeth Hoekstra: Oh, yeah. I will revisit all of these things when I have the power and the money to do so. I will be knocking down doors, and all of Detroit's schools will be different.

UPDATE: I want to share this amazing update with all of you. Recently, I found out that shortly after the work we did with the goal of rebuilding the Detroit schools, in 2018 the city raised funds to be able to install water filtration systems at the schools. Rumor has it a fuss someone made about the kids and the risks they faced finally started to come out - haha 😊. The schools still need to be rebuilt, which is something I am definitely addressing in the future. Back to the interview*

Regina Meredith: I definitely see you're going to be doing that in the future.

Elisabeth Hoekstra: Oh, for sure. It's not fair for our youth to have to go through things they're not even conscious of. Destined for failure.

Regina Meredith: For kids, you don't have a chance in these environments; your parents didn't have a chance and maybe even their grandparents.

Elisabeth Hoekstra: Yeah, not a chance. And you know, the way politics is set up, I won't speak out on it too much, but it's not working.

Regina Meredith: No, it's not working. It's going to take warriors and warriors like you to come and beat down the doors and change it, and you'll do it. I see you're going to do it.

Chapter 18

The First Modality

Regina Meredith: So, meanwhile, your personal life, now, you had started connecting, also now, let's move into because it has an interesting little kind of crossover period where you're thinking, "Hmm", the mind, you're starting to do some neurofeedback for example. But you're using it as a crutch still because you still have other things; the habits hadn't been completely put to bed yet. So, let's talk about your first encounter with neurofeedback. Neurofeedback is powerful. I've done it myself, different modalities through the years. It's powerful stuff. So, how did you find out about it, and what happened when you first started experiencing it?

Elisabeth Hoekstra: So, when I first started neurofeedback, which is now, wow, fifteen years ago, I found out about it through my friend that got killed, TC, his neighbor.

Regina Meredith: So, this was way back when you were in the midst of all this stuff—drugs, partying, criminals.

Elisabeth Hoekstra: Yes. Interestingly enough, I always was conscious of self, and I always was trying to be better and get better, even though I had the dark parallel of my drug habit.

Regina Meredith: The duality within you was so extreme but powerful.

Elisabeth Hoekstra: Yeah. So, as soon as I found out about it, I thought, "Wow, I'm going to try this. It sounds fun. Let's do it". So, that night, I actually went and I trained, and wow, it brought me out of this fog I was in for years because of the drugs. It was hard for me to even complete sentences at the time because of all the drugs I was taking; my brain was fried, literally. I mean, eight ecstasy pills in a night, you can imagine. So, it brought my speech back, and, "Wow, this is great". It changed my life for a little bit, but I still was going back to the same environment full of drugs and alcohol. I started using neurofeedback as a crutch throughout my time of crazy, which I think helped me not fall all the way off.

Regina Meredith: Absolutely. Yeah, and it was a wise decision. You didn't know exactly why you were compelled to.

Elisabeth Hoekstra: It always made me feel better from being hungover, which is not how you should use neurofeedback at all, but at least I didn't fall off the deep end. So when I watched Tony Robbin's special and something clicked in my head for me, that's when I made a decision, a conscious decision, I'm going to be better, and I'm going to change. I'm going to be positive. I felt good. I felt good naturally. And so, I changed my thought process, which took a couple of steps to completely shift. I started waking up and writing in my journal, which I hadn't written in over twenty years because my mom had found my diary when I was a teenager and read it.

Regina Meredith: You probably needed help for that.

Elisabeth Hoekstra: Oh man, it was one of the worst experiences in my life. So, it traumatized me and I stopped writing. I was a huge writer when I was younger. I started writing for the first time again when I was trying to change my thought process, which helped me. Something about the pen to the paper is different than anything else, typing, everything. I remember I was doing affirmations all the time in the mirror. I would stand in the mirror and tell myself all of these positive things.

Regina Meredith: Good old school stuff.

Elisabeth Hoekstra: Oh man, my self-esteem was so low because I just got out of the relationship with the narcissist. I thought I was the ugliest, dumbest piece of shit in the world. I drastically needed to build my self-esteem back. So, I would stand in front of the mirror, naked. "I am beautiful, I am intelligent, I'm smart". It took a long time for me to believe these things. The process helped my mind frame. And instead of listening to music, I started listening to books and podcasts. I started reading a lot more as well. I would drop my son off at school, and on the way to drop him off, we'd listen to affirmations, and I'd make him repeat them with me. So, we'd be in the car, repeating affirmations, repeating affirmations, and every time we'd go on long road trips, affirmations. So, that really helped me and hopefully helped him as well. I remember I was on a trip to a real estate convention in Hollywood, Florida, and I took some of my team members, and we went out there. We went out to a club, and I think I was still taking drugs and stuff sparsely and doing a little bit of drinking and stuff at the time. And for some reason, it hit me like a ton of bricks, "I just don't really need to do this anymore". And so, from that day on in 2017, I made the conscious decision. I'm not going to do drugs, and I'm not going to drink alcohol anymore.

Regina Meredith: How long ago was this? How many years ago?

Elisabeth Hoekstra: About five years ago now.

Regina Meredith: You went Cold Turkey off of everything.

Elisabeth Hoekstra: Off of everything.

Regina Meredith: And then, you really started busting your butt on the therapies.

Elisabeth Hoekstra: Yeah. More so than I had already been throughout my years, but this time, taking everything much more seriously.

Chapter 19

Boundaries

Regina Meredith: So, I want to talk about this a bit, because up to this point in your story, people will be able to kind of dip in and say, "Oh, I've been in that situation" or, "Wow, I always wondered what that was like", but understanding ourselves through your story. You are a great experiment of healing modalities, so people can start seeing what might work for them as well. So, we've got neurofeedback. Go a little deeper on what the experience of it was that really made you resonate with it, and then, in order of what helped you, let's look at some of the other modalities.

Elisabeth Hoekstra: Neurofeedback took a lot of anxiety away, anxiety I didn't realize I had until I saw the contrast following a session.

Regina Meredith: When you start seeing which portions of the brain are trashed and way over-amped or have low energy, and how out of balance the various portions of the brain are, It's intensely powerful and useful.

Elisabeth Hoekstra: It is very, very much so. And when I was nineteen, back in the day, I actually got my brain mapped.

Regina Meredith: I was working with Lee Gerdes at Brain

State back in 2006 with the neurofeedback system created, but the therapy started taking off after that, and you found one of the people accredited in his process, and at the machinery.

Elisabeth Hoekstra: Sure did. And, you know what? Those brain maps blew my mind, but they also showed me the brain can be stuck in a state that will cause you to act out. It will make you act in ways you would not do consciously, or if the blood flow was normal and your brain was firing in the normal way it's supposed to, you wouldn't have all these crazy wants, and you wouldn't be doing all these crazy things. For most of my life, I felt like I was frozen on the inside.

Regina Meredith: Frozen, but no sense of consequence. No long-term view of what happens next.

Elisabeth Hoekstra: Zero. And that showed up in my brain map.

Regina Meredith: And how does it show up? What's that look like in your brain map?

Elisabeth Hoekstra: So, he mapped me, and he told me I was way on the fight or flight end. And then, a couple of weeks later, he mapped me again, and I was in a deep freeze. Usually, a person is either fight or flight or freeze. My fear center was also completely shut down.

Regina Meredith: You're not swinging gently between the two poles.

Elisabeth Hoekstra: Exactly. I was swinging off the deep end, and I think that's been part of my defense mechanism. I go into freeze when I experience major trauma, but I'm normally more on the upper, fight or flighty side, you know? But when serious traumatic things happen to me, my brain goes into complete freeze; shuts off, and I turn into a doll. I don't know where I go at that point. So, it all showed up in my brain map. When I started training, my brain started becoming more balanced. And especially when I got off the drugs and alcohol, brain training, among other things, really brought me into balance because I was not self-soothing anymore; I was not going into toxic environments to bring me out of balance anymore. I was sticking to the sober life and also cutting out and creating more boundaries in my life.

Regina Meredith: Yeah, let's talk about boundaries because you had made some, well, some would say, questionable choices in partners, but they were a match for what you're trying to learn. So, what happened when you had to start making different choices in the people in your life? I want to talk about your parents too.

Elisabeth Hoekstra: So, when you don't have boundaries, you have no real self-love. You let people run over you, you hate yourself because you have no respect for self. You let people do whatever; you're a feather in the wind. When I started becoming conscious and falling in love with who I was, I realized, "I can't let these people treat me like this or talk to me this way. This is crazy". I stopped letting people pull me in all these different directions. And my group of friends changed a bit because a lot of them were on drugs and everything else. They shifted out of my life because now, I want to be positive, and I don't want to be around drugs and alcohol, and I don't want someone to be in my house, high, anymore. I didn't want to be around any negative energy anymore. I wanted to be sober and be around people who are feeding me, who are pouring into me, instead of me pouring into everybody else with nothing in return. I wanted to be around people who lift me. And so, I cut a lot of people out, and I stopped letting people run over me.

Regina Meredith: So, that's a critical step. And I remember one time a friend of mine said, "Hey," and I was at a kind of low point in life, and she said, "You've got to go to this thing. Just go to it". So, I signed up. I didn't know what I was going to do. It turned out to be eight days of something like minds, wellspring, or whatever those groups are based after, but the one thing the person taught people in the eight-day period of pretty brutal exercises was, "Your associations are 90% of what your life is going to look like". And, so what you said there is indicative of that.

Elisabeth Hoekstra: Oh yeah, absolutely. I mean, it shows up in your life too. Being in the energy of a drug addict, that's coming onto you, even if you can't see it, the energy is still there. We're bioelectric beings; we're picking up everything, frequencies from everywhere. If there was a fire at the other side of the house, the energy from that would be picked up. So, your group of friends and the people you spend time with, you're them; your energies are intertwined all the time. So, my life changed drastically when I changed the people I was around.

Chapter 20

Trauma Stuck in the Body

Regina Meredith: So, you had to change your people, now, you're able to get your brain, and one of the things about various forms of neurofeedback, the net effect is if you have anxiety in life in general, it starts knocking down the anxiety because it brings the hemispheres in balance with one another. It's really beautiful.

Elisabeth Hoekstra: Yes, it is. I had insomnia for a very long time, and sleep is so important. I remember when I started neurofeedback and grounding regularly, my insomnia started going away.

Regina Meredith: So, that's what you were doing to your brain, but you also started doing bodywork, and you had one practitioner—Mindy in particular, who's able to help you. So, let's talk about what happened there, because now, we're getting down into the stuff from when you were little, even.

Elisabeth Hoekstra: Right, yes. So, when I was always focused on more of the brain, and I had always done neurofeedback all throughout my toxic years, I never addressed the body. When I started getting very, conscious I started doing the bodywork, I then realized how much trauma is held within the body.

I started going to a bodyworker regularly. She's certified in all different types of bodywork; over twenty different things she's certified in. This lady is something else. But she focused on SomatoEmotional release work on me. She basically connects to you on a cellular level and connects to cellular consciousness. She will put her hands on you and feel in her body what you are going through, or what is in a specific part of your body, or what type of trauma, where you hold your trauma. I mean, it's crazy. The first time I went to her, I knew she was good because she put her hands right over a spot that pulsates when I get angry; literally, it becomes painful right on my chest.

She put her hand right there, and as soon as she put her hand there, I wanted to start bawling, crying. I don't even cry in front of people. I've never cried in front of people throughout my whole life.

So, I started bawling, and I'm like, "What is this?" throughout my sessions, but I knew something happened there. Something seriously drastic happened there for me because my body has been through so much trauma in my life. So many people's bodies have been through so much trauma. What people fail to realize and what medicine has failed to realize and teach us is about the mind-body connection.

Every thought, traumatic experience, all of these things, you store it inside your body. Then, if you don't get rid of them, they manifest physically as cancer, tumors, or an autoimmune disease. Everything manifests physically in your body if you don't properly process it. Unprocessed trauma leads to reactivity and inappropriate outbursts of emotion. Going through and doing this bodywork, it's been so healing for me. Sometimes she'll put her hands on me, and memories I stuffed down will flash through my mind, and with her help, I'm ready to process those memories. I mean, my whole life has been choppy, and I've blacked out a lot. There are years I've blacked out. I feel for good reason, your higher self won't let you process anything your mind and body can't handle.

Regina Meredith: There's a grace in that. Nothing's really allowed to be seen until you're ready to see it.

Elisabeth Hoekstra: Exactly. But with the help of her, I needed something to really—

Regina Meredith: To facilitate that.

Elisabeth Hoekstra: Yes, and I've noticed a drastic change. I used to have terrible road rage, awful, and now, it doesn't phase me, not at all. I had it so bad I even shot at a person's tires before. I used to be up-down, up-down, and especially with my son, I could get overly angry, and I would get the pulsating pain in the first spot Mindy had worked on. The anger issues I initially thought rose from D, the narcissist, I come to find out came from years and years of compiled trauma.

Bodywork, being sober, and finally becoming conscious of the trauma I endured, I realized the extent of my anger. The massive amounts of anger lay underneath the surface where I stuffed them year after year after year. I never cried in front of people. I was in deep freeze, probably most of my life. I literally never, never cried, ever.

Now, when I work with Mindy, I'll be bawling on her table sometimes because she's connecting to cellular memory. It's uncontrollable. It'll just come out, the tears, but it's good. I need it to come out of your body. The suppressed emotion needs to be felt, expressed, and released.

Regina Meredith: Well, yeah. And we talked about this at the beginning of our talk, and that is, if we are carrying the DNA of our ancestors in our aura, those are pixels of who we are, our emotions, our thoughts, etc. What was in your mother and what was in your grandmother? What had they endured and put up with that was in you by the time you were born? No less all this other trauma heaped on by yourself.

Elisabeth Hoekstra: Exactly. Keyword, on myself. So, I realized a powerful point in my consciousness journey, I made myself go through everything I went through.

Regina Meredith: Oh, yeah, we are the architects of our lives.

Elisabeth Hoekstra: Exactly. And I'm not saying it's right for any person to rape another or to do anything wrong to anybody.

Regina Meredith: And I want to say as a caveat too, absolutely not. There's no excuse for people abusing other people. But on a soul level, there's something in us trying to balance out and get rid of, maybe transform is a better word. Something in us that would allow ourselves to sink into a state of despair and self-loathing and to be humiliated to the extent where we have to wake up as you did.

Elisabeth Hoekstra: Exactly. Well, you put yourself in situations, and you surround yourself with the energy. So, coming to that realization and really owning my own trauma, it's a very powerful place to be because no one can do anything to me anymore. I've done it all to myself.

Regina Meredith: And you already had this other highly functional, talented, intelligent part of yourself that was developed and still developing. And so, it's not like you had no ground to stand on once you realized that. You weren't just like, "Oh, if I'm not the world's victim, what am I? Well, I'm successful at this, this, this, this. I'm a lot. I'm a mother".

Elisabeth Hoekstra: Yeah. A powerful place to be. Just coming into more awareness, in a state of more awareness, and doing the bodywork and doing the different modalities I realized I needed to address certain things with the people I wanted to keep in my life. And I've noticed, throughout my life, I had a lot of resentment for my mom, and it's hard for me to talk to her. It was always hard for me to talk to her without an attitude, you know? And so, I became conscious of that. And I considered, "Why do I have this attitude speaking to my mom? She's never turned her back on me". And so, I had to dig and find out there were things in my childhood and adult life triggering me that I was holding on to still.

Chapter 21

The Scary Conversation

Elisabeth Hoekstra: I knew I had to have a real scary conversation with Mom. So, I sat her down one day, and I expressed the scary stuff I kept inside that I thought I would hold for the rest of my life because I didn't want to have that awkward conversation with that person.

But it took me so much strength to sit with her and tell her, I feel like this about this, and this made me feel this way. The conversation alone was healing—to hear her perspective of things. It made me forgive her for a lot of things where I thought she was just, "Screw you". Her perspective shined a whole new light on my life. She just loved me. All she wanted to do was protect me. It wasn't her trying to do anything wrong to me or my dad trying to do anything wrong to me. They were doing the best they could with what they knew how.

Then, they also kept a lot from me I didn't even understand in my younger years, you know? Foster care was coming after me, which is why they sent me to boarding school. She worked within politics and worked within the system, and she knew what happens in foster care. She didn't want me to get abused again. So, they made their decisions for real intentional reasons.

Having those hard conversations with people, especially your parents, if you've gone through things, is a powerful thing to do and very healing. So, that was a big step for me.

Regina Meredith: Beautiful. So, that was your mother and your father. So, you came to understand because you were mature, you were clean, you were able to hear it. Any other primary people you needed to reconcile with?

Elisabeth Hoekstra: You know what? I've done a lot within myself. There are some people who can't have a healthy conversation, like the narcissist. He broke me; he broke me so bad it led me to become conscious, I think. That much pain endured over the years will eventually wake a person up. I had to heal the heartbreak and brokenness within myself, which took a lot of self-processing and self-building. I had to forgive him, really forgive him.

I had to forgive a lot of people within my own being, not for them, but for me. The process helped me a lot to move on from certain specific relationships and certain specific people I held on to, and from the anger, I had to release my anger and learn to forgive, learn to understand how everybody is doing the best they can with what they know.

Regina Meredith: And that's basically it. We're all flawed. We're all here and dancing between the forces of light and dark; higher realms and lower realms; beings from all places whispering in our ears. The little devil on one shoulder, angel on the other, you know, it's the human condition. And it's just who you want to listen to, really, inside yourself. And so, you did acupuncture, you did floatation, I mean, you did kind of, every therapy out there, but then, ultimately, your own ingenuity kicked in, and you created, what was it? Sound healing?

Elisabeth Hoekstra: Yeah. Sound, frequency, and vibration. That's everything; that's all that we are. That's all that's here. When I started digging into information, which is one of the first stages of awakening, the information stage where you gobble up any knowledge you can get your hands on. While there, I researched vortex math, the pyramids, ancient history, neuroscience, anatomy, the list goes on. Everything was mind-blowing to me, and I couldn't stop indulging in the information. When I was getting into sound frequency and vibration and how important those things are, I started trying to create something within my mind because I was working at a wellness center focused on mental health, and there were specific modalities there. So, we were creating different programs to help people go there and benefit the greatest from what we had.

So, I started experimenting in my mind and thinking about certain things, and yeah, it was a sound bed. I wondered, "What if this resonance goes through your entire body and your body starts resonating at certain positive frequencies; would that do something? So, after researching the topic a bit, we found it should create a positive effect in the body. So, we created a sound resonance bed, and yeah, it vibrates to specific frequencies, and it's thoroughly relaxing, and it puts you into a meditative state almost immediately. So, that was really cool.

Regina Meredith: So, do you have it for yourselves, or do you guys have a business doing this?

Elisabeth Hoekstra: Yes, we actually sell them for home use at the company I'm currently at.

Regina Meredith: Oh, wonderful. Well, that was a nice contribution to your last job. So, I'm sure your mind's already spinning on some other things.

Elisabeth Hoekstra: Yes. Working there opened up my eyes to a lot of different holistic modalities, more so than I already was open to. I started really digging into bio-hacking, trying to hack my physiology and be optimal at all times.

Chapter 22

I Am Grateful

Regina Meredith: So, what are some of the key things that you discovered that really helped you get back in and stay in balance on a mind-body, literally, on a brain chemical level, which affects the emotions and body?

Elisabeth Hoekstra: Routines are very, very important. For me, especially, but I think for everybody. When I'm sleeping and I wake up, I think of five things I'm grateful for immediately before I think of anything else.

Regina Meredith: I love that. That's my favorite.

Elisabeth Hoekstra: That really retrains your brain too.

Regina Meredith: It retrains it; it goes into gratitude, appreciation, beauty, remembrance. It's so powerful.

Elisabeth Hoekstra: Yes, it is. And it's really something to start your day with that power. And for a while, I had to write it down to really feel it, but now, I can repeat it in my head. That's helped me a lot. I'll get up, and I'll meditate in front of Red Light Therapy.

Regina Meredith: Yeah, tell me about that.

Elisabeth Hoekstra: Oh man, Red Light Therapy, it's everything. It helps you with cellular regeneration, increased mitochondrial function and ATP, enhances collagen, and so much more. So, it helps your body heal faster, and it gives you energy, not that I need anymore, but it's a lovely modality. It's helped me a lot. Because I have that routine, when I sit in front of Red Light therapy, it immediately puts me into a meditative state. I don't even need to think about meditating because I trained my body and my mind to quickly go there as a habit. The routine caused my brain and body to know, "Okay, we're sitting in front of Red Light therapy, it's time to meditate", which really, really helped me. And meditation alone is amazing. It's crazy the number of thoughts we don't even know and recognize as there. And the only way that you can find out that they're there is—

Regina Meredith: To try to silence them.

Elisabeth Hoekstra: Exactly. So, meditation was big for me because I was able to dump a lot of those excess thoughts, and it helped me become more present and more conscious. And after that, oh, the rebounder. I have this rebounder; it's a Cellercisor actually, by David Hall, and each spring in the Cellercisor is specifically rotated to work every cell in your body. So, that's very beneficial for your lymphatic system. If you have a stagnant lymphatic system, that's your life force energy, the fluid in your body gets very stagnated, and then you get kind of tired or exhausted; your energy isn't flowing. And if your body fluids are not flowing, it's just a fractal of your energy, so your energy is not flowing.

When I started working on my lymphatic system, it was a game-changer. I actually met a girl, her name is Mysteek, she was giving me manual lymphatic massages for a while, and I noticed an obvious change. It made me way more positive. I started to feel almost high, with no drugs. Oh man, I felt so grateful all the time for everything, I was all—"Oh, I just love everybody and everything".

I made working on my lymphatic system a really big part of my life because of the massive change in my whole being, my whole attitude, and my overall energy levels too. I used to get tired every single

The Recipe to Elevated Consciousness

day around two-three o'clock. But now, I can just go, go, go because I feel like everything is moving and circulating in my body correctly.

So, every day, I'll do a little bit of lymphatic work on myself. You can even use a toothbrush. I got that one from Dr. Perry Nickelston who teaches how to do all types of different things for your lymphatic system that you can easily do at home. Between that and jumping on the rebounder, the Cellercisor, really, really works your lymph.

Working my lymphatic system made such a great impact in my life I invested into a body suit—The Ballencer Pro (FDA approved)—that is made specifically to work the lymph. You put it on and it inflates and deflates with air gently working your lymphatic system. It works bilaterally and circumferentially so you really get a full work up with it. Learning about the lymphatic system and applying it into my day to day was a major contributor to positive change in my life.

And then, something that's probably one of my favorites, I jumped levels with grounding. Oh my gosh, when I found grounding, it changed everything for me, everything. I used to not respect the Earth as much. I mean, I used to love Mother Earth, but not like how I do now. It's like, I can't see a piece of trash on the ground; it breaks my heart. I can literally feel my heart breaking inside me. It's like, "Oh, how are we doing this to our mother?" And I really think, and I can attribute that back to grounding because grounding connected me back to mother earth. We're bioelectric beings.

Regina Meredith: Yeah, the frequencies of mother earth.

Elisabeth Hoekstra: Oh man, we need to be connected. And in the 1960s, '70s, they invented synthetic shoes, and they slapped rubber on the bottoms of our shoes and disconnected us from the free electrons that are all over the Earth's surface that our body needs, literally needs these. If you see a graph of shoe sales, diabetes, and autoimmune disease, you'll see all three of these things increasing equally. It goes up along the same scale.

So, when I got reconnected to mother earth again, my whole life changed. I could take deep breaths again. I was never able to breathe into the bottom of my belly button, and being grounded enabled me to do so. Breath is so important with everything meditation, energy in general, thought process. I started working on breath because finally, nothing was blocking it. I notice my nervous system really, really calming down every time I'm grounded, and my sleep is way better. I never wake up with pain anymore, which from gymnastics, I used to wake up with lower back pain every single day. From being grounded, I wake up with zero pain in my body. I ground my son, and he's very connected with the earth. He never used to be, but now, he'll get upset if there's trash on the ground as well.

Regina Meredith: Yeah, that's powerful.

Elisabeth Hoekstra: Oh man, it is. And I noticed it's balanced my circadian rhythm. I wake up at the same time every day, even if I'm six hours ahead in another country, if I ground myself out there, no jetlag. My circadian rhythm just syncs back into that part of the earth. So, that's how powerful this is. That created leaps for me.

Regina Meredith: Oh my God. So, you could do a little self-help video just on healing modalities, your personal experience alone.

Elisabeth Hoekstra: Oh yeah, for sure.

Chapter 23

Helping the Masses

Regina Meredith: So, then you met Billy Carson. We're here at his house right now, and you started collaborating together. It turned out, you're able to really start kicking in that whole notion of being able; how do we position ourselves in the world to be our best so other people can see us and hear us and want to engage with us? That is a huge talent and skill you have.

Elisabeth Hoekstra: Oh yeah. It was very interesting how we met. We met through my last job, which is one of the really amazing things I take away from that job. I'm so glad I was able to shift my life positively after I met Billy. He hired me into his company, which is amazing because everything he's about and does, I believe in 1000%. He works like a hundred men, and he's just one. I knew I could provide more structure and lend some helping hands because he does it all himself, everything. I mean, 13,14,15 businesses he runs.

Regina Meredith: That is insane. His ingenuity, his energy, his intelligence, and brilliance. It's crazy.

Elisabeth Hoekstra: Oh yeah. It blew my mind, and it's hard for people to blow my mind, but he did from the moment I met him.

A true blessing. So, I took my skillset of seeing where there are holes and provided detail and structure and a new look and grabbed attention from different places. Coming from all the different careers I had, I made a lot of connections. And you know, his brand is very niche. I told him, "You got to get out to the mainstream. Everybody needs to know what you have to say". So, I came in, and I organized things so he's able to really use his full brain power, use all his knowledge to be the visionary for his company and to spread to the masses. All of this backend stuff, I'm trying to systemize everything, so he has more space to do and speak to the world, which he should be doing all the time, pushing the brand more mainstream.

Regina Meredith: And from what he says, you're doing a brilliant job, which is lovely. So, let's hop down the road. You're still a young woman, you've packed lifetimes into one, but you're still a young woman. What do you see for yourself? What is your greatest— and like you said, social injustice, you're going to go kick doors down, your greatest passion, and are you starting to connect with who you are and what you're here to do?

Elisabeth Hoekstra: I've almost died so many times, which leads me to believe I'm meant to do something important. I want to share my story to inspire people, women, mostly young women because I can relate to a lot of negative instances young women go through that are pretty common. I want to inspire ones who may have or may be going through what I did. I want them to know you can go through things, and you can still make it. You can still become a powerful business person, you can still be out here helping the world, changing the world, and you can be doing it while you're happy, actually happy; not fake happy, not on-drugs happy, not alcohol happy, but really, truly from your soul, from the bottom of your stomach and your heart, happy. You can get out of all of these negative situations and change your thought process around and change your life around and do what you're meant to do, which is align with your divine purpose. In order to do that, you have to clear all the trauma; you have to go inward and focus on self.

Regina Meredith: You can't assume it's going to go away by brushing it under the rug. You took a lot of time, a lot of resources, and commitment to go through all those healing modalities to get where you are right now.

Elisabeth Hoekstra: Right. Shedding layers and dropping the trauma, you can find divine purpose. I know my divine purpose is to spread awareness and help the world become more conscious. What we've been doing, it's not working, and I feel like we can enter into a golden age and be full of only love and light.

In my head, I always said, "I'm here to help massive amounts of people", because, in order to change the collective thought process, you have to affect massive amounts of people. Because right now, the energy and the collective, it's not in a good place. You see it manifesting in your day to day on the earth.

Chapter 24

Aligned with Purpose

Regina Meredith: So, after all of this, I mean a lifetime, you've crammed lifetimes into this short life that you've had thus far, you've learned so much, you have so much will, so much intelligence.

Elisabeth Hoekstra: Thank you. I've aligned with my purpose. I feel like it's almost impossible to do when you're filled up with stress, trauma, and you haven't dealt with yourself. By going inward and dealing with my inner turmoil, falling in love with myself again, and shedding all these layers of picked-up trauma, epigenetic trauma, and everything else I've experienced, I feel aligned with my divine nature. Nothing grabs and pulls at me like it used to. I've shed major layers.

Regina Meredith: We forget our emotions are energy fields, those realms of us are intertwined with those realms of earth. So, what we feel, this is being projected back to us by earth. Not with herself. Look what happened to her in COVID; she healed herself. The skies went blue, the foxes started roaming the streets of the cities. It was amazing. She doesn't have the problem, but she's suffering our problem.

Elisabeth Hoekstra: Our problem. Exactly. And I feel like she's sad, and her sadness is emanating back within us.

Regina Meredith: It's a feedback loop now.

Elisabeth Hoekstra: It is. And until people can face themselves and see themselves and step out of whatever mentality they're in, the collective is in, whether it be fear, anxiety, depression, and address within themselves—I mean, that's really the only way I feel the collective will massively change, is to address their own issues, go within and get into alignment. Which always falls within love because our spirits, we're love at the baseline of everything, and our love should be what's manifesting in this earth instead of wars, trauma, stress, and anxiety.

Why are people shooting each other? The collective is so stressed out right now. I see it with the pandemic, all these crazy crimes happening, everything is manifesting from the collective. So, people need to take responsibility and gain their power back from all the trauma and stress they're dealing with within themselves. When you change and become aligned, you naturally step into light and love, which emanates around you, eventually changing the people around you.

Regina Meredith: Absolutely. And you brought up a couple of points, which I'll go ahead and kind of tap into; you can give your own reflection. One of them has to do with you saying, "Yes, we have to enter, we have to create a world where we're all loving, etc. We have a lot of influences on this planet from above and below. We can go in any direction we choose. There is a video called, *By After Skool*, it's on YouTube. They did one recently on a mass psychosis; how it sets in and what's going to be required to take us out, and what it is. Is this connecting multi-generationally through the heart with each other? And as they called it, and I totally agree, creating parallel societies. We may not be able to take the banking structure to a healthier level, but we can create our own economy. And this is what you're really a genius in, in a sense. Building. I mean, even though it started

The Recipe to Elevated Consciousness

with some kind of dodgy deals, but you knew how to create an economy.

Elisabeth Hoekstra: I like to create working systems, and systems out of love, instead of capitalism. Billy says, "Take capitalism out of healthcare". You have to. When you look at everything, there's enough money to go around, enough resources to go around for everybody to be abundant, everybody. But the thought processes are messed up.

Regina Meredith: I agree. And in the interim, it's not going away. Nobody's going to give up their stuff right away. We have people with massive amounts of control and money. They're not going to give it up. But slowly, but surely when we unplug from the game and create our own parallel societies, there's nothing left for them to use anymore, so to speak. And so, not to be discouraged or afraid because it seems overwhelming; we have to do this, each of us, one at a time.

Elisabeth Hoekstra: Yes, one at a time. Exactly. Because even though you think you're only one person and, "What am I going to do?", I had that thought process before, but you would be amazed at what you're capable of.

Regina Meredith: You can, especially you. Now, you can go kick doors down to get healthier living conditions for children, or someone else might make the most beautiful cakes in the neighborhood and make everyone feel joyful and happy. This is all of value and part of creating a healthy society.

Elisabeth Hoekstra: Yes. It absolutely is. Everybody has purpose. It's being able to align with your divine purpose, and not ego purpose, and not what they said your purpose is, but really, going within, healing all the turmoil, doing the hard inner work, and taking your power back and realizing what's for you and your creativity; what truly makes your spirit happy.

Chapter 25

Expanded Consciousness – The Future of Children

Regina Meredith: I read an article about the head of FED, and they said, "Look, this is a fact, we have to find our way back, but we're never going back to the pre COVID economy". And it was said in an interesting way, he said, "all these kids, their lives have been altered, and they're having to find their way out of it. And they're going to become a creative generation and offer incredible solutions". It was kind of interesting for humanity, and you have a little boy.

Elisabeth Hoekstra: Oh my gosh. And kids are so resilient. I don't think we give them enough credit. It's very traumatizing the stuff they've been through, but they're so resilient. And I think even throughout this huge trauma, everybody has experienced and some are still going through it, we're going to grow stronger if we take our power back and open our eyes a little bit to see what's going on. What's REALLY going on. I mean, we're already starting to see it with the creativity of the young twenty-year-olds and the teenagers. They are open to more, and I think that's a major thing we all need to address, is be open. Stop judging.

Regina Meredith: Listen to these kids. They're smart.

Elisabeth Hoekstra: They're smart and they're more intuitive. They're less closed off to the bigger picture, and everyone needs to open their eyes a little bit and see the bigger picture.

Regina Meredith: I agree. I think there's definitely hope, and I think this isn't something that's just going to happen in a decade or in a lifetime, even, but the changes will start now. They are already starting; some amazing things are already in motion.

Elisabeth Hoekstra: I see it. I see consciousness, I've seen more people becoming more aware, and I'm proof. I've noticed for myself, I've done the hard work, I've done the inner work. And because I've aligned with who I'm supposed to be, I'm already creating change for whoever I'm in contact with, and that's just me; I'm just one person. Imagine ten people doing the hard work and taking their power back, and finding their divine purpose. They'll create massive change. And there are groups of people they touch, and it'll keep growing and growing. It's exponential, and then the change becomes the collective instead of what it is right now.

Regina Meredith: Absolutely. I couldn't agree more. Any final thoughts before we say goodbye? This has been such a fascinating and inspiring couple of hours to spend with you because you've had such a different trajectory from two middle fingers up to authorities with badges on, they've just blasted into your space, to coming to a place of, we have to join to together in love.

Elisabeth Hoekstra: I really hope people were able to relate to my story. Know you can go through things; you can go through massive trauma in your life. You can keep on attracting massive trauma in your life, but you can change it all. You can turn it all around. You can live your best life, your dream. When I was younger, I didn't think I could ever be this happy, I didn't think I could ever be a fun person without drugs and alcohol, and I didn't think I could ever feel whole. But I can tell you right now, I've never been happier, and I've never felt more whole in my life. By going inward and addressing yourself, and standing up against whatever it is in you causing you to shut things out or feel frozen or anxious—the grass is greener on the other side.

Regina Meredith: There are so many rewards. You have so much going on in your life, and you have a beautiful little boy who loves you to pieces.

Elisabeth Hoekstra: Yes! And he does. And I can honestly say I feel better now than I ever felt on any type of drug, on any type of alcohol, at the hottest red-carpet parties. I mean, I would take this clear-headed, euphoric feeling, immediate manifestation power, 10,000 million, gazillion, infinity times over any of those things in my past I thought were everything.

Regina Meredith: Well, you earned it; you did the hard work. Thank you so much, Elisabeth. You're an inspiration with a fascinating story, and I can't wait to see what you're going to do with the rest of your life.

Elisabeth Hoekstra: Thank you.

Regina Meredith: You're going to do many powerful things.

Elisabeth Hoekstra: We'll see. We shall see. Thank you so much. It was a pleasure.

Regina Meredith: For me too.

Elisabeth Hoekstra: Thank you.

The Modalities

In this crazy, fast paced, and toxic world we live in, it's hard to live optimally without the help of different tools and tricks. I always knew I wanted to FEEL better, but I never knew how to achieve this. I didn't have much hope after my young years full of people telling me things like, "Just stop thinking that way" "You'll get over it" "Time heals all". None of these sayings helped me at all. Time didn't heal all my wounds, I did not just "get over it", and I couldn't control my thoughts to "stop thinking" the way I did.

I experienced my first modality at nineteen, now sixteen long years ago. This sent me on an upward trajectory seeking to find more knowledge than I knew possibly existed about these holistic modalities. Even though it took some years to commit to my healing process fully, I felt hope for the first time after that day I spent brain training when I was a teenager. I experienced for the first time since birth what it was like to SEE clearly and consciously.

I didn't dive into bio-hacking when I first experienced it all those years ago because I wasn't consciously ready to commit to the lifestyle. Being a bio-hacker IS a lifestyle and you have to be ready to commit honestly, seriously, and fully to really gain all the benefits the lifestyle reaps.

There were MANY ups and downs in my journey, which has made the ride so amazing for me to live. Bio-hacking involves lots of experiments on yourself to see if it works for you or not. What is good for me, may not be good for the next person. I actually almost killed myself one time by trying a new hack. About five years ago, I read about doing a liver/gallbladder flush and wanted to try it. I read the instructions, got the ingredients, and went for it. I made myself so sick and dehydrated, I was down for days. I was in so much pain I could not get out of bed. Once I worked my way back to health, I researched what had happened to me. I mistakenly got the wrong kind of magnesium for the detox and ended up overdosing on it. Not fun. But I learned my lesson, and now I do heftier research before jumping into a new bio-hack. This lifestyle takes dedication; that specific instance could've scared me away from bio-hacking, but instead, I dove deeper.

I've done OVER fifty different modalities during my span of bio-hacking the past seven years. Some have worked better than others, some have not worked at all, and some have completely shifted my life. The only way to know what works for you is through trial and error. There were many times throughout my healing journey that I wanted to throw in the towel. There were days I got so excited about a new modality just to find out it wasn't right for me or didn't do what it was supposed to do. I've spent thousands and thousands of dollars on different therapies I wanted to experience. Still, I would not change anything about what my bio-hacking journey has brought me. The benefits GREATLY outweigh the shortcomings.

I want to tell my readers to take the first step, to just TRY one thing. See how it shifts you. Don't get defeated if it doesn't give you the result you want right away, either. Some modalities take a longer commitment, and you'll see the benefits over time.

The Recipe to Elevated Consciousness

A lot of the bio-hacks that I share in this section don't have immediate results or even results that you will feel. Sometimes, I'll commit to something and expect the results right away, and to my dismay, it will take months. Or I won't even feel anything, but what I do notice, and call tell you, is that you'll see the result within the new life you are creating—that's how it's been for me.

I look back through my life and see the ways in which my lens changed significantly since I started bio-hacking. My perspective is different, my mind is clear, and I've shed the layers that created the void within, the void I filled up with drugs and alcohol.

Not only will I continue to bio-hack my best life, I will continue to inspire others to do the same in every way I know how. This lifestyle turned my life completely around, and I know it will do the same as well for anyone that commits to it. Give it a try, and don't give up!

Chapter 26

The Brain Dump

Neurofeedback is a powerful, life-changing therapy. The modality provided me the necessary contrast for hope—hope to feel better, hope to get out of the mind state I was stuck in, hope to get my brain back.

At nineteen years old, I was stuck on stupid coming off a pretty hefty ecstasy and Adderall drug binge. I couldn't even complete full sentences, which was not a good place for me to be as I always prided myself on being naturally smart. Terrified my mind would never come back, I was in a constant state of awkwardness feeling "cracked out".

I remember the following moments as if they were yesterday because the whole trajectory of my life altogether changed. My best friend—TC, RIP, lived next door to a practitioner experienced in brain training, specifically Brain State*. Neurofeedback helps to balance the brain and bring our nervous system into a calm and relaxed state. My habit of continuously looking for something to optimize my mind and body kept me open to pretty much anything. So, when TC introduced me to the practitioner, John, I signed up to go that same day.

My full trust being in my best friend, TC, I left with John, to an office to try neurofeedback for the first time. Surprisingly, I was more excited than nervous. I anticipated this to be something that would benefit me, I could feel it, and by the way John's eyes lit up when I volunteered to come train, I gathered this could in some way be profound.

At the office, John led me downstairs to a small room with one chair and a bunch of computer screens. My nervous excitement increased tenfold as I sat down. John measured locations on my skull and placed sensors in specific spots. He then put headphones on me and told me he'd be back in twenty minutes to change the sensor placement on my head. I laid back in the chair and tried to relax my mind as John instructed. While distinctive musical tones played, I wondered how this would ever help me.

After six days of training every day for at least two hours at a time, I found myself making drastically different decisions. My new direction uplifted my life instead of adding to the trauma in which I was engulfed. My brain fog was almost gone. From the drug-induced dream state that I couldn't get out of, I shifted to a clearheaded, motivated, and ready to take on the world state of readiness.

In addition, I slept a healthy number of hours and woke up rested. I made healthier choices with food and working out. The depression cloud that hung over my head since childhood gradually lifted.

For many years, which I HIGHLY recommend AGAINST, I used brain training as a crutch to support my partying and drugs. I went out in the evening, drank a bunch, popped a couple of pills through the night to keep the party going, and woke up the next day in a complete fog. Still foggy, I headed to train my brain. Afterward, no more brain fog—completely normal again.

Now, I continue to do neurofeedback/brain training whenever I need support. Since I first experienced neurofeedback all those years ago, they have come out with all different types of brain training. I have tried all different types of neurofeedback, and I would recom-

The Recipe to Elevated Consciousness

mend everyone to do their own research on them before experiencing it or deciding which is best for you. Over time, I learned to tell when I'm off and when this therapy can help bring me back. I plan to utilize this modality for the rest of my life.

https://www.ncbi.nlm.nih.gov/pmc/articles/PMC4892319/

https://www.ncbi.nlm.nih.gov/pmc/articles/PMC4892322/

*Brain State, founded by Lee Gerdes in 2004, is an advanced neuro technology that rebranded in 2018 as Cereset®. Cereset provides brainwave optimization technology that helps to balance your brain and bring your nervous system into a calm and relaxed state.

Elisabeth is ready to begin a session of brain training.

Chapter 27

The Secret to Relieving Pain

The first time I put on a grounding patch, I took the deepest breath I have ever taken in my life. Without delay, my nervous system calmed down and I shifted from sympathetic (fight or flight) to parasympathetic (rest and digest). For the next couple of months, I continued to use all the grounding products I ordered—patches, sleeping mats, a pillowcase, blanket, headband, and a meditation chair. My sleep tremendously improved.

I fall asleep almost instantly upon hitting the bed now that I ground. Instead of my usual restless habit of waking multiple times throughout the evening, I now soundly sleep. Even though I endured excruciating back pain from years of gymnastics, the plague of pain I experienced almost every morning ended. I now wake up in ZERO pain.

Let me go into the science a bit for a better understanding of what grounding/earthing achieves. To be grounded means we are in direct contact with Earth's surface, allowing the transfer of negative ions into our bodies. There is an abundance of free electrons all over our planet from continuous lightning hitting the ground and these negative ions are necessary for the human body to function optimally.

Before synthetic shoes that disconnect us from the healing powers of Earth's surface were invented, humans were always connected and grounded. Since we slapped rubber on our feet, there has been an enormous increase in autoimmune disease, diabetes, and the list goes on. When the body is ungrounded, the body's inflammation increases, which tends to be the root cause of autoimmune disease. So, until we are grounded—either by touching the Earth's surface directly with our skin or through a conductive material, or connected to a grounding device, we carry a more positive charge in our bodies which isn't ideal for health.

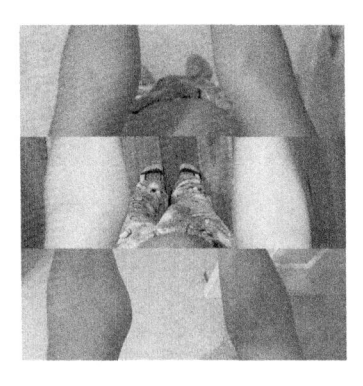

The bottom picture shows Gabriel's left arm after a spider bite. Away from home, his arem remained swollen for five days. I took the middle picture six hours after putting a grounding patch directly on the bite. The top picture shows twelve hours of wearing the grounding patch. The inflammation is completely gone!

Grounding is also great for endurance during workouts. The first time I benefited from this increased shift in energy occurred on a hike through the woods with my then 7-year-old son. I wore moccasins made of leather, which is a conductive material, and the negative ions from the earth's surface transferred straight into my feet. I am not, nor have I ever been, a runner. I am good with quick sprints and heavy lifting, but I have never been effective at long runs and cardio. With the obvious extra energy in my body, I wanted to experiment and see how far I could jog. To my son's surprise, who had never seen me do such a thing, I started running. To my astonishment, I remained unwinded. I jogged faster and faster until I achieved a medium running stride. I couldn't believe it. I ran through the woods, up and down hills, and I breathed perfectly without my usual windedness or even feeling tired. I probably ran that day for a

The Recipe to Elevated Consciousness

mile or more, which I hadn't been able to since nearly a decade and a half ago while in high school. This is the power of grounding!

Speaking of my son, he is now nine years old and quite mature for his age. He respects the earth, has an even keel attitude, listens to directions, and isn't hyperactive which is so common in children these days. I attribute a lot of this to the fact that he has been grounding alongside me since I started. Grounding brings your body back into a state of homeostasis which calms the nervous system and helps the body to relax. Earthing now has over twenty case studies proving the science behind the benefits of it.

Lastly, I want to mention the benefit grounding gives to our circadian rhythm. Traveling with a client of mine on a work trip, we flew across the country. We went from the eastern time zone to pacific—a three-hour difference. Usually after a long day of flying, I am fairly out of it and exhausted. When we landed, we went straight to the hotel and the first thing I wanted to do was ground. The patches I brought with me stick directly on the skin and connect to an outlet to provide the electron transfer. Five minutes later my energy returned to normal. The exhaustion and fog that clouded me from the plane ride disappeared.

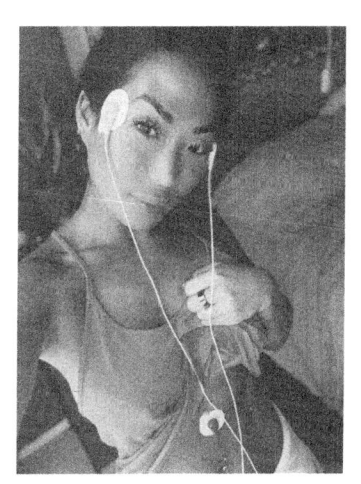

Since I can remember, my migraines were so bad they made me vomit. I would be down for days. Now, if I feel a headache coming on, I put patches on my temples, and I feel almost immediate relief. I love sticking a patch on my solar plexus as well.

That night I put one patch on each foot in the K1 point. This placement assures grounding throughout the meridians of my entire body, so I usually sleep with the patches in this position. The next morning surprised me. Like clockwork, I woke up at my normal 5:45 a.m. even though I was in a totally new time zone.

Since then, as I travel the world, the first thing I do when I arrive in a country is put my bare feet on the ground or head straight to an outlet so I can ground. Diving into saltwater is also an amazing way to ground as well, so if there is a body of water around, I'll definitely jump in that. This decision made MASSIVE, positive, change in my life.

https://www.dovepress.com/the-effects-of-grounding-earthing-on-inflammation-the-immune-response--peer-reviewed-fulltext-article-JIR

https://earthinginstitute.net/wp-content/uploads/2016/07/Cortisol-Study.pdf

Scan this QR code to go to Earthing.com

Chapter 28

My Place of Zen

Climbing into a floatation therapy pod for the first time, my heart raced with excitement. Already deep into bio-hacking, I researched this modality long before the opportunity for experience arrived. Floatation therapy wasn't popular at the time, so when a local wellness center brought a pod to metro Detroit in 2014, it was the first of its kind anywhere in Michigan.

I slowly stepped into the pod. Once settled into the 1,000 pounds of Epsom salt dissolved into one foot of water, I was immediately addicted. Not only does floatation therapy provide our bodies with the necessary magnesium transdermally, but the sensory deprivation provides a much-needed rest for our busy western society's brain and body. As a fast-paced culture, we never give our brains' a chance to shut off and eliminate the unnecessary gunk that we don't even take notice of because of our jammed-packed schedules. Not being able to clear these excess thought patterns from our minds has been slowly killing our awareness. No space for thought process = reactiveness.

Floating effortlessly in skin temp saltwater, with zero noise or light, brings up what needs to be processed. The therapy allows the brain and body to go into a state of deep relaxation which produces theta waves in the brain. When the brain is in this frequency, you can even reprogram your subconscious mind.

I have enjoyed many wild experiences in floatation therapy. I've astral traveled, saw myself in past lives, had instances I was able to manifest almost immediately into my life, and even experienced a visual of my birth to find out the time I was born. Magic happens when we shut down the stimulus and are fully present with self and only self.

https://www.healthline.com/health/sensory-deprivation-tank
https://www.myfloatzone.com/casestudy

Chapter 29

An Unexpected Rush of Emotion

About three years ago, I realized I stopped hitting new levels of optimization. I hit a plateau in my bio-hacking journey. That changed following a divine intervention that brought me to experience an extremely intuitive and talented practitioner named Mindy.

Due to extreme trauma experienced from a very young age, I learned to disassociate from reality—freeze. This disassociation caused me to forget huge portions of my life.

Every year my anger kept getting more difficult to suppress, to the point it was spilling over in inappropriate ways—road rage, attitudes, snappiness, reactiveness, and explosive fights with my ex. I needed more healing but had no way to reach the next level. For a couple years of my life I feared nothing could help me, until I met Mindy. Mindy played a HUGE role in my growth starting in 2019.

I walked into the dark, small, cozy little space, and from the first session my life changed.

The session started with me barefoot. Mindy stood behind me and put her hand on my head. A rush of energy went from her hand all the way down my body to my feet. I could literally feel this sensation physically. The energy revealed a heaviness in my heart chakra in the same space where I often noticed the radiating physical pain from anger during moments of outrage.

Next, Mindy instructed me to lay down face up on the table. Promptly, she put her hands over my heart chakra where I felt the heaviness of that physical pain and energy. I was ecstatic. Mindy knew where my body needed help, and her hands rested on the exact point.

SomatoEmotional Release Body Work turned out to be exactly what I needed to reach my next level of healing. I continue weekly to fit in at least an hour or two of body work. Each session is unique. Sometimes the hand placement brings back different memories that require processing and emotions to be released. At times, I laid on that woman's table and cried like a banshee, and yet other times the hand placement brought nothing into my consciousness. The higher self always knows what's best for the conscious mind. When nothing comes up as Mindy's hands are placed on me, I believe this is an internal protection mechanism the higher self uses to hide the things I'm not ready to consciously process.

What I do know is that when I started doing this type of body work my anger dissipated. I no longer deal with road rage, I've gained massive awareness of my physical being and the trapped emotions stuck in different areas, and I live a more pleasant and conscious life. I have Mindy's talent to thank for breaking through the plateau I hit. She helped me rise to the next level of my healing journey.

As always, when choosing a practitioner, do your research. This type of body work takes years of practice and intuition that is only gained by doing the work on SELF, followed by extensive professional training, and supported by an ability to stay constantly aware. Find an experienced individual that you are entirely comfortable with and can truly trust. If you are working with someone that does not know the intricate details of whatever body work you're receiving, or that you are not entirely at ease with (especially specifically with SomatoEmotional release work), this hands-on modality becomes much less effective and can even be detrimental to your mental and physical well-being.

https://www.healthline.com/health/mind-body/how-to-release-emotional-baggage-and-the-tension-that-goes-with-it#How-to-release-emotions-from-the-body

https://www.ncbi.nlm.nih.gov/pmc/articles/PMC5518443/

Chapter 30

Everyone Needs an Outlet

I have been in talk therapy nearly all of my life on and off. A good therapist can help mirror back to me my own issues and traumas and help create a safe space to work through those experiences. There is something achieved by verbalizing things aloud so the brain can hear. The reflective listening and sharing that occurs helps me to overcome seemingly impossible blocks.

Personally, I found that sometimes I simply need to vent about situations that would be otherwise inappropriate to speak to anyone about. Having this safe and comfortable space with a therapist I trust has helped me let go of numerous issues and events.

When looking for the right therapist for you, it's important to first figure out your intention of going. What goal do you want to achieve by seeing one? For me, I wanted to make sure I could relate to whomever I was talking to, so I looked for one that was the same race as me, with some of the same experiences I had. It took me a couple of different appointments with a couple of different people to find the right fit for me.

Chapter 31

Stay Spiritually Connected

My search for the "thing" the "person" that could help me understand myself better began at an early age. I believe I was only twelve when I had my first psychic reading. I was always so interested in psychic abilities, tarot cards, and other supernatural methods. My spiritual advisor, Cortney, and I commenced our work in 2014. She supported me through traumatic events, the death of many people who were close to me, accompanied me with different energetic rituals, and assisted as the vessel for me to check-in and connect with my guides and angels. Having someone I could talk to for reassurance knowing I'm on my path was truly a benefit.

https://cortneykanesides.com

To provide a visual experience for her clients, Cortney paints throughout their sessions. Each picture is unique and reflects what comes through during the session.

Chapter 32

Protect YOURSELF

One of the early signs of change and my ability to know the shadow work helped came when I put in place healthy limitations. Boundaries create more self-love. Before I walked down my healing journey, I lived without these protections in my life. The abuse I sustained as a young child taught me the opposite of healthy boundaries. I learned to submit and do what I was told so people would appear to care for me. This led to a life of trauma and drama as my lack of self-worth and wanting to please everybody put me in so many negative situations.

There are levels to this healing journey. I always find myself interested to watch others "wake up" because I witness people cross each phase of consciousness, and one of the biggest for some is the swing from zero boundaries to ALL the boundaries. I was so protective of self when I found love within, there was absolutely no chance during that time I would allow myself to be put in any situation that might bring me pain. Too protective, but that's what I needed to do at that time in my life to move forward with my healing.

Boundaries protect us from hurting ourselves and having resentment for others. This is big. I didn't recognize this until later in my life when I realized the amount of pent-up anger I held towards a couple people who treated me terribly. Well, people only treat us the way we allow ourselves to be treated. Without boundaries in my relationships, I ended up getting treated absolutely awful and holding resentment and anger towards the perpetrators for years. This only hurts the self, by the way. Forgiveness is a benefit to the person who is doing the forgiving as we release old stale emotion and animosity. Within even very healthy relationships, there must be boundaries established to prevent bitterness and resentment from creeping in.

Boundaries help others to respect us, because if we don't respect ourselves, how can anyone else? If I don't love myself, how can anyone else? Create healthy boundaries and watch the resentment directed towards others dissipate out of your life.

Chapter 33

Heal Your Relationships

Healing relationships is a bio-hack in itself. This is because people in your life, especially your partner if you're in a relationship because you spend large amounts of time with this person, affect your biology. People actually stimulate biological responses in the body to release different hormones which make each person interact a certain way. These secreted compounds greatly impact our mental health and influence whether our minds and bodies are in a stress response or not.

When we learn our triggers and find out the roots of our behaviors, most of the time, these relate back to our parents. From birth through to age seven, our brain/subconscious is being programmed. Any unwanted programming that occurs can cause lifelong issues and often does as no human is perfect. Parents make mistakes. Unfortunate situations that can result in negative programming present themselves throughout childhood. No one gets out "scot-free".

One of the hardest conversations in my life was the one I needed to have with my mother. There was so much within my past that had shaped the way I was, starting with the adoption trauma that led to a reality of constant abandonment. My parents tried to do their best, only to end up cutting that wound deeper instead of helping me heal. I was left alone while having tantrums, sent away to boot camp and boarding school, sent away to families' homes I didn't know while my parents took care of my brother in the extensive hospital stays he had to go through because of a kidney issue, and all this aggravated and added to my feelings of abandonment and low self-esteem. Add on the sexual abuse I experienced as a young child, there were issues I needed to iron out with my mother. To heal those parts of my inner child, I needed to create a clear, safe space.

After months of contemplation over whether I would have this awkward and difficult conversation I finally decided to pull the trigger. Thank God I did. Our communication was powerful and sharing our journeys helped me to understand my mother's perspective. I found clarity and understood so much more than ever before. This lifted a ton of the lifelong resentment I carried. The energetic weight literally rose off me after that conversation.

Having those hard conversations and airing out what we may have kept buried within our memories is one of the most transformative bio-hacks we can achieve in our lifetime. Not only does the process heal us, but our communication also heals the relationship we have with others. Whether we choose letting go or moving forward, the conversation is an important step. Remember, everything emotional that we carry affects our physical in some way, shape, or form. The more awareness we have of individuals and why people evolve one way or another frees us of our own pain, and gives us empathy, instead of judgment.

Chapter 34

What the Body is SUPPOSED to do After a Traumatic Experience

Trauma Release Exercise was founded by a brilliant and inspirational human named Dr. David Berceli.

"TRE® is an innovative series of exercises that assist the body in releasing deep muscular patterns of stress, tension and trauma. The exercises safely activate a natural reflex mechanism of shaking or vibrating that releases muscular tension, calming down the nervous system. When this muscular shaking/vibrating mechanism is activated in a safe and controlled environment, the body is encouraged to return to a state of balance."

Learn more on:
https://traumaprevention.com/

Whenever we experience trauma, we ALWAYS intertwine with our physical in some way. Getting these emotional cuts and bruises out of the body is necessary. Notice how animals in the wild do not have PTSD. They eliminate trauma directly after it happens. When animals are attacked, they fall to the ground and shake, then stand right back up like nothing ever happened. The damage does not stay in the body. Just like animals in the wild, we need to use a trauma release method to do the same thing.

    I was introduced to TRE in 2015, and I was not ready. I tried the method but felt so goofy that I couldn't receive the healing the modality offered. Not until about 2018 did I seriously reconsider this practice. With the help of a certified trauma release trainer walking me through the steps, I immediately realized success and how much benefit the process provided. My energy grew less anxious in my body, I slept better, and enjoyed an all-around calmer existence.

    I do NOT recommend this exercise without the help of a certified trainer. The one time I did trauma release by myself, I flooded my system. I had a HUGE discharge of energy to the point where my whole body was convulsing off the ground. I was hysterically crying and couldn't calm down. Memories were flooding my head and the only way I was able to stop the flow was through the next modality known as the Emotional Freedom Technique—or EFT.

    https://traumaprevention.com/

    https://www.ncbi.nlm.nih.gov/pmc/articles/PMC4268601/

Chapter 35

Tap Tap Tap

Thank goodness for EFT—Emotional Freedom Technique AKA tapping. This bio-hack was the only thing that helped bring me out of the exorcism I created by doing TRE without a professional guiding me. One of the simplest hacks available, EFT is so effective and doesn't cost any money.

Each tapping point has multiple releases and allowances. Tap under the nose to release embarrassment or fear of failure. Tap to allow self-acceptance and compassion.

Tap the chin to releases confusion and allow for clarity.

Tap the collarbone to activate the adrenals.

Tap under the arm to allow clarity and confidence.

By tapping on different energy points on the body, we send signals to the part of the brain that controls stress. Stimulating these areas unsticks emotion and stress to be processed. Disrupted patterns return to normal.

I fall back to EFT if I am stuck in a negative emotion about something and can't seem to bring myself out. Using this modality can reprogram thoughts, actions, emotions revolving around certain traumas and so much more.

I can use EFT for something as simple as feeling bad about a negative comment someone writes about me online to something as complicated as reprogramming emotional reactions attached to childhood abuse.

I even taught this technique to my now nine-year-old son who started tapping at age five. This is an empowering hack for kids!

https://www.ncbi.nlm.nih.gov/pmc/articles/PMC6381429/

https://www.healthline.com/health/eft-tapping

Chapter 36

It May Look Funny, But the Results You Get...

This modality greatly assists with meditation. The device looks funky, but the outcome is crazy. I connect the Brain Tap device to an app on my phone, then put the device on my head, and sit back and listen to the music while a gentle light stimulates my retina.

When I tried this, my meditation instantly became more effective, allowing me to achieve a relaxed state of mind, and then move into the connection to oneness very quickly. This device appeared to guide me to a multidimensional plane where I received universal and personal downloads. Brain Tap is a frequent addition to my meditations.

> "Our BrainTap Headset brings a whole new dimension to your brain tapping sessions by adding the restorative power of light frequency therapy. In addition to the sonic effect in the audio sessions, the BrainTap Headset delivers gentle light pulses that travel through the ear meridians and the retina, sending direct signals to the brain and guiding you into extraordinary brain states

that would otherwise take years of disciplined effort to achieve."-Brain Tap

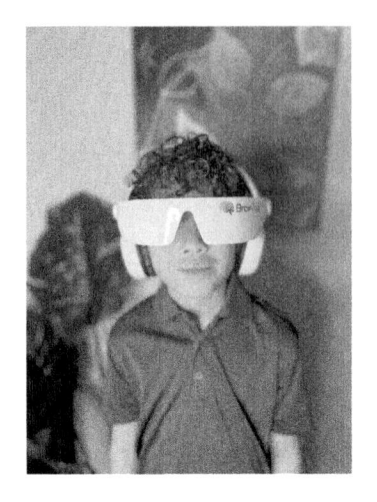

As you can see, the brain tap device rests on your head with headphones over your ears and a visor over your eyes. Once connected to your phone, this technology provides different protocols depending on the result you are trying to achieve.

"In addition to the sonic effects, the BrainTap headset delivers gentle light pulses that travel through the retina and ear meridians, sending direct signals to the brain and guiding you into unparalleled brain states."

"Pulsing light, in the correct pattern and intensity, can produce levels of deep relaxation known to affect serotonin and endorphin levels, with an average increase of 21% in one study. These increases not only can calm and relax the mind but also produce powerful effects in maintaining a positive outlook and optimistic thinking."-Brain Tap

https://braintap.com/

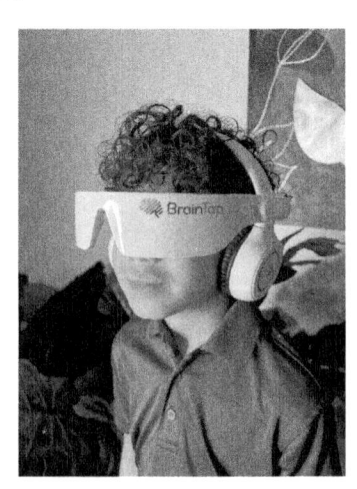

Chapter 37

Pins and Needles

The first time I received acupuncture was to quit smoking at age fifteen. I remember after the treatment ended the cravings decreased significantly. The first cigarette I smoked after the session tasted awful, I just wasn't ready to fully commit to putting the cigarettes down. Since that time, I continued with acupuncture because I appreciate the effectiveness offered towards balancing me out.

My recent sessions of acupuncture have been focused on decreasing anxiety and becoming more grounded. After each, a sense of calm takes over my body. I also notice a slight euphoria that lasts a bit after the treatment completion. This is a therapy I want to utilize for the rest of my life.

https://theacademyofacupuncture.com/clinical-case-studies/
https://pubmed.ncbi.nlm.nih.gov/28483186/

Chapter 38

A Simple VIBE That Can Shift Your Whole Mood

A wearable device, Apollo Neuro sends a vibration and frequency into the skin, which directly influences the nervous system. The wearable unit has several settings, from energy and wake up, all the way to deep relaxation and sleep. I knew that this device was greatly effective when one day I had a bad headache making me extremely nauseous. I put on my Apollo set to "Rest and Recover", which is designed to specifically help headaches, among other things. I achieved almost immediate relief,

Apollo Neuro worn on my left ankle provides me the best results.

which isn't normal as my headaches quickly turn to migraines. This tool also comes in handy for focus. One of my favorite settings is "Clear and Focused", which I have on right now. This useful device keeps me dialed in to any project I'm working on. I love the sleep mode as well, which literally feels like the vibration cradles you into deep relaxation.

This is one bio-hacking tool I take with me everywhere. The device can be seen in pictures I post. I often see comments of people laughing because I appear to be wearing an ankle monitor. No, I'm not on house arrest, hahaha. The apollo is most effective on the inside of either wrist or ankle and I wear the device on my left ankle because I have found I get the best results with that placement.

Here I am in Egypt wearing the device to keep my energy high during the intensive climbs through the pyramids.

"Apollo Neuroscience was born from research at the University of Pittsburgh. Drs. David Rabin MD, PhD and Greg Siegle PhD worked with each other at the Program in Cognitive Affective Neuroscience to develop and scientifically prove out the Apollo technology.

Together, these researchers discovered that certain combinations of low frequency inaudible sound waves (vibration that we can feel but can't hear) can safely and reliably change our sense of touch, and that we can measure those physiological changes in near real time."

Read more on:

https://apolloneuro.com/pages/science

Chapter 39

Coherence That's Necessary

When trying to function optimally in this dimension, heart and brain coherence holds immense importance. A huge part of my growth, practicing Heart Math measures my body's Heart Rate Variability or HRV. HRV tracts the variation time between each consecutive heartbeat.

The simplest way to measure if my autonomic nervous system is sympathetic or parasympathetic—fight or flight, or rest and digest— uses Heart Math. We now know that signals not only go from the brain to the heart, but the heart to the brain. When the heart is in coherence, a body is relaxed, and cognitive function is high. When we are out of coherence, our body goes into a fight or flight state, with parts of our brain getting less blood flow, leading to loss of cognitive function.

When the autonomic nervous system is in a sympathetic state, our heart rate increases. When this happens, the variation time between beats holds a steady, regular rhythm. When the autonomic nervous system is in the parasympathetic state, our heart rate decreases. Our heart then beats to meet the body's needs but without a regular rhythm. The lack of a regular rhythm causes our HRV to increase. When we have a higher variation time between beats, this generally means our body is recovered and things are functioning properly. When our HRV is lower, this generally means our body is in a more stressed state, and we need to give ourselves time to rest and recover.

The device I utilize clips on my ear and attaches to my phone; my HRV is read while I breathe deeply, focused on breathing out of my heart chakra. To breathe from the heart chakra, picture literal breath coming in and out of the center of the chest. Take in love and light, and breathe out old, stagnant energy. Strive to focus on the energy and breath going in and out of the heart, and how that feels within the body. The reading shows the level of my heart-brain interaction, and HRV, revealing if I am in coherence or not.

https://www.heartmath.com/science/

Chapter 40

Embrace The Full Spectrum of Emotion

This topic is a biggie for everyone. We came to this world with our senses to help us navigate around this matrix. Throughout history, we've been taught that "negative emotion" such as anger or sadness is not good. How many times have we heard "Stop crying, man up!". Young boys especially are taught not to express emotion. Emotions are human/equal and supportive of our journey. Emotions are not negative or positive, emotions just ARE. Until we learn to freely experience our full range of emotions, we won't grow as a society. Stuffing down emotion creates a life of turmoil, puts stress on the physical body, and sometimes causes major mental health issues. There is only so much space where we can stuff our emotions until we can't hide them anymore. I'm the perfect example of this.

Throughout my life, I would teeter back and forth between freeze and fight or flight. I would go from emotional extremes to disassociation. I remember when I went to jail and absolutely nothing scared me. I wasn't even upset, I was just there, and life was like a dream. I faced real time, and I couldn't conjure up any type of emotion about my situation. I wore the attitude of, "Screw you, do what you want to do. I don't care", and on the surface, I honestly didn't care. Little did I know, extreme turmoil boiled inside me subconsciously, while my nervous system was stuck in deep freeze.

Over the years after stuffing and stuffing and stuffing my emotions, I eventually turned my emotions all the way off. I didn't have a care in the world, which allowed me to live an extremely dangerous and risky life. I subconsciously created drama for myself in my attempt to FEEL something. This caused more trauma to pile on what was already a mountain.

I remember my constant drama led to fights with my physically abusive boyfriends. Being stuck in a dissociative state made me fearless. I egged them on saying things like, "Kill me then, I dare you". I wasn't outwardly scared of anything, but that's because I couldn't cross the subconscious wall I created to separate the hurt and traumatized little child deep within me from my hardened exterior.

All this "unfelt" and stuffed emotion eventually started to spill over. I would have crazy bouts of fury triggered by my ex, who we'll call D. Originally, I thought the bouts of fury came from my anger towards D. What was really happening, though, had nothing to do with D and everything to do with me. I began to open the anger I pushed down since BIRTH and man was there a TON.

There was a specific instance where I knew I needed to find outside help with my anger. I was driving on the highway after a huge fight D. The fury took hold of me, and I literally lost control of myself. I furiously sped like a mad person without a care in the world almost wanting to die, wanting to FEEL the pain of an accident, wanting to FEEL something; anything. I got home and proceeded to beat my car up. I cracked my dashboard, split my hand open, and kept going until I broke nearly everything in my car and was too exhausted to continue.

I destroyed my car because I never got congruent with how I deeply experienced myself on the inside. I had so much excess energy stuffed in my physical body that needed to release in any way possible. Fortunately for me, that day my car got the grunt of my anger, instead of an actual person. I didn't kill myself, or anyone else, which I'm so grateful for, as my emotion during that instance took me over completely. Murders and suicides happen when people are in these states of uncontrollable emotion.

I was always the happy friend, the bubbly one, the strong one that never cried, and the one that my friends would dump on with their problems because I always had the answer. I wasn't "supposed" to be upset ever; I was supposed to be positive. Because of my forced control, I bounced between not showing anything but happiness, and deep freeze—disassociation until I couldn't anymore. Finally, my physical body was so filled up from unresolved trauma, my emotions started to spill over inappropriately. I completely lost my ability to perform my "happy" act.

Emotion compiles over time. Once I learned to be okay with my sadness, to embrace my anxiety, and honor my anger, all the stuffed emotion could finally dissipate. To be able to really move through tough situations in life, we must learn to deal with things as they come up. Now, I let myself cry, I feel my emotions deeply within my physical body, and I honor that I'm having this experience. This is a beautiful thing. I don't view any emotional response as negative or positive anymore, they just are what they are and I'm grateful I can finally feel all of them.

Denying emotion is to deny self.

Chapter 41

The MAGIC Tea

With the use of this transformative plant—"Magic Mushrooms" AKA psilocybin, I definitely healed some previously untouchable traumas. I knew I held trauma associated with my birth. I wanted to know exactly what happened the first couple of months of my life to figure out where my extreme fear of abandonment and feelings of unworthiness stemmed from.

That's the intention I went in with as I drank my tea. I laid down on my grounded bed after I drank my cup and closed my eyes. The next four hours would set the positive trajectory in which I would release one of the biggest traumas in my life. As I reached the peak of the medicine's influence, my entire life, all memories, all moments could be seen parallel to each other. I could look upon every moment in my life at the same time, because where my mind went to, there was no such thing as "time". I reexperienced my birthing process. I journeyed through every emotion of the experience from the age of me as a tiny newborn. As soon as I was born, I was pulled away from my mother. I never saw her face. I never looked into her eyes. I never felt her arms around me. The staff carried me away and placed me into a crib. I stayed in that crib for the first three months of my life, being monitored. Caregivers didn't know the importance of physical touch for babies back then, so we were basically fed, and watched. The physical interaction was slim.

Connecting the memories of my first moments in this life helped me understand why I am the way I am. The awareness alone brought me deep healing, knowing I wasn't crazy for the feelings I have known I felt since my first breath in this world. The awareness alone will profoundly impact your mind and body. Dig for the awareness of those root issues within your trauma, it is so powerful.

https://www.hopkinsmedicine.org/news/newsroom/news-releases/psychedelic-treatment-with-psilocybin-relieves-major-depression-study-shows

https://www.ncbi.nlm.nih.gov/pmc/articles/PMC6007659/

Chapter 42

Rid the ENERGY VAMPIRES

We are who we surround ourselves with. I make sure what I encircle myself with is serving my greatest good. If we allow negativity into our space, negativity is exactly what we create in our life.

As soon as I cut the negativity, cut the toxic friends, cut the toxic relationships, cut the energy vampires, my life became peaceful. Before I cut these ties, I attracted drama into my life. Subconsciously, the behavior fed a trauma pattern I had, the need to always exist smack dab in the middle of something crazy.

These days, I can't even remember the last time "drama" entered my life. I refuse to allow the interruption anymore. I have created a safe, peaceful, healing space for myself throughout this process, which is necessary when processing trauma and unresolved emotion. Shadow work leaves us extra vulnerable and very open to different energies; being around a lot of "unhealed" people, can leave us thoroughly drained and feeling awful. After all the years of drama and trauma, I'm proactive in the protection of my space and whom I let in. I only invite energy that feeds me, fills me, and leaves me inspired after every encounter. This has manifested peace, harmony, and expansion in my life. I won't give that up for anyone.

Chapter 43

Drugs, Alcohol, Sex, Shopping, OH MY!

You are either in alignment with the divine, or you are stimulating to sustain misalignment.

Read that again.

You are either in alignment with the divine, or you are stimulating to sustain misalignment.

Throughout the course of my life, I utilized resources to distract me from my pain. I was always surrounded by friends, at the hottest parties, I kept myself engulfed in busyness. I used stimulation from any source I could find to escape the fear of taking a hard look at myself.

This avoidance of slowing down created a life full of addiction and unconsciousness. I was too busy for any type of thought process. I would even distract myself in the late hours of the night online shopping to avoid thinking about what was happening in my life at that time. Each of us might find this behavior in the most subtle things we do. In those moments when we catch ourselves in whatever the distraction of our choice might be, pay attention to any anxiety or unease present within the body. Direct attention there to see what the REAL issues might be underneath that distraction.

Overstimulation or imbalanced attention happens when we use things to distract ourselves from issues so we don't have to "deal with" or "don't have to think about" it. This behavior is us using stimulus to run away from root issues that need to be addressed. Stimulation can be shopping, eating, having sex, partying, doing drugs, working too much, really anything. Make sure to become aware of these things and address the real underlying issue if there is one.

It takes a strong person to face issues head-on as they arise and evolve with their emotions every step of the way. Be strong. Stop turning a cold shoulder to distract yourself. I promise on the other side of what you're running from, comes true peace and harmony.

Chapter 44

Emotional Ties to Traumatic Events Re-Shaped

My introduction to EMDR came from a friend of mine who had gone through terrible family trauma. The horrific events included his stepdad killing his mother then killing himself, his brother committing suicide, and his other brother getting brutally murdered. All of these tragic events happened on or near the holidays which makes the experience even MORE traumatic. The fact that EMDR therapy helped him process through, live through, and survive these tragic events immensely influenced me to move forward with this modality.

Fortunately, my therapist since 2012, had trained in EMDR. For the session, I sat down in front of my therapist with two clickers, one in each hand. We went back in time to traumatic events that took place in my life, and the devices in my hand would vibrate back and forth as we verbalized through these events.

EMDR reprograms the emotional tie we have to a traumatic experience. I left the session that day a bit loopy and a little confused. I took that evening to integrate back to stability, but the day after, I felt amazing. My repetitive thoughts and emotion tied to the event we processed with EMDR dissipated and no longer held the same intense charge prior to my session. EMDR is effective if performed by a trained practitioner.

> "Eye Movement Desensitization and Reprocessing (EMDR) therapy is an interactive psychotherapy technique used to relieve psychological stress. It is a treatment for trauma and post-traumatic stress disorder (PTSD)."

https://www.healthline.com/health/emdr-therapy

Chapter 45

Stop Chasing Pain – Lymphatics with Dr. Perry Nickelston

One morning I was surfing Instagram and came across an extremely unique page that instantly grabbed my attention. This IG was full of information about a body system that I didn't know much about—the lymphatic system. Unfortunately, when I attended school in the 90's and early 2000's, we didn't learn much about one of the most important systems in our bodies.

Perry Nickelston of @stopchasingpain is a Chiropractic Physician with primary focus on Performance Enhancement, Corrective Exercise, and Metabolic Fitness Nutrition and trained from The American College of Addictionology and Compulsive Disorders. He specializes in the lymphatic system and has an approach to the body that is unique from the "normal" way of medicine in Western culture.

During 2019, the morning I found this amazing IG page, I began my journey with lymphatics. I immediately reached out to network with him and plan a time I could receive a session. Since my first session, each treatment I've experienced since then has benefited my life incredibly.

The lymphatic system is responsible for getting rid of the toxic waste within the body. Sounds important to me! This system's job is to transport lymph, a clear fluid that runs throughout the body. While serving multiple functionalities as part of the immune system and the circulatory system, cleaning out the toxic waste is the system's most important job.

After I received my first three manual lymphatic massages, I experienced a brand new me. A sense of euphoria enveloped me, and my life seemed brighter. The open flow of lymph and energy supported a growing feeling of gratitude for everything in my life.

Eastern medicine recognizes lymphatics as the vital Qi energy, and to reconnect to your Qi means reconnecting to our life force energy. I definitely agree with their belief as after I started working on my lymphatic system, I connected much more with my body and life force energy.

https://www.livescience.com/26983-lymphatic-system.html
Dr. Perry Nickelston
@stopchasingpain
https://www.stopchasingpain.com/

Chapter 46

Jump Around to Work the Lymph

Rebounding is a great way to move lymph. Any type of jumping does the trick. For me, I use the Cellercisor, by David Hall. This specific rebounder is designed for working our lymphatic system using springs that are specifically coiled to work every single cell in the body.

Rebounding is a great way to move lymph. Any type of jumping does the trick but for me, I use the Celleriser, by David Hall. This specific rebounder is designed for working our lymphatic system using springs that are specifically coiled to work every single cell in the body.

When I first got my rebounder, I was following the included workout protocols. I ended up getting my six-pack back after ninety days of consistently working out on it. It always pleases me when I can SEE results after I start doing something different. My energy has stayed up, my mind/body feels clear, my back pain doesn't visit me anymore, and my circulation has increased. I can tell this is a fact as I don't have cold hands and cold feet anymore, which used to be an issue for me.

I love this modality not only for myself and the results I received from it, but I also love it for my son. Parents, I would suggest getting one of these. He's been jumping on that thing since the day I got it; he was five. Now nine, it's helped his energetic-self dissipate some of that pent up energy. Anytime he gets a bit rowdy, I'll tell him to go jump, and not only is it great for his health, but he's also able to calm himself with an activity—double win!

"The Cellerciser® uses the patented TriDaptable® spring that offers support, movement, adaptability, and lift. It's the only self-adjusting spring of its kind, adjusting to the weight of the person using it and to the height that the person is jumping. It stretches from the middle, and the weight is gradually absorbed as needed through the tiered-tapered ends allowing the body to accelerate and decelerate smoothly and safely with added support. Most other rebounders use little tube springs that can cause nerve damage, knee problems, and lower back pain."

Learn more on:
https://cellercise.com/about-cellercise/

Chapter 47

Brushing Isn't Just for Your Head Anymore – Lymphatics

Dry brushing is not only tremendous for the lymphatic system, it also is good for building up collagen within the skin. Getting rid of dry, dead skin, helps circulation, and if done often enough, can even eliminate cellulite.

When you dry brush, you should always brush towards your heart, from the top down, and from the bottom up. You want to do this because it moves the lymphatic fluid to where it needs to go to be cleaned and circulated properly. Remember, if you don't move, your lymph doesn't move, so brushing is an amazing way to stimulate this flow.

There are specific brushes for skin brushing. They are usually thicker bristle brushes so they can really stimulate your skin and lymphatic fluid that sits just under the surface of it. These brushes are also an exfoliator and they are a great way to get that top layer of dead skin off. I now love dry brushing and do it often.

I've witnessed my skin tighten on my body, and even the shape of my body changed. My stomach got flatter, and my waist got smaller. This makes sense because consistently moving that stagnant fluid to process through your body, cleans your system and decreases inflammation. I love the way it feels on my skin, the way it makes my skin look, and how I feel afterward—which is usually energetic and happier.

This is definitely one of the less expensive modalities that if you stay consistent with can make a very positive difference in your life.

https://health.clevelandclinic.org/the-truth-about-dry-brushing-and-what-it-does-for-you/

Chapter 48

Plunge Right In

Cold Plunging is a great way to kick start your lymphatic system. When we immerse our bodies into cold temperatures, our blood vessels constrict causing lymphatic fluid to be pumped through the body.

My life in Michigan, where winters are freezing, left me completely disinterested in this experience. Still, I found the effort to train my mind and body to want this VERY difficult bio-hack. I would turn my shower temperature to icy at the end. At first, I could only stay in the water for about half a second before I couldn't take the freezing sensation anymore. As I kept repeating my effort, I continued to increase my time in the cold water. After about a month, I could stand in the freezing water without it even really phasing me. Through the process, I observed a drastic change in energy levels. When I took my freezing cold showers, I sustained much more energy and focus.

There are other options for cold plunging other than taking cold showers. Some facilities have hot and cold plunge tubs that are designed specifically for your lymphatic system. This is one of the most efficient ways to move your lymph as blood vessels constrict and open pumping fluids through your body, improving circulation. When your body is warmed, and then shocked with cold temperatures, this activates the sympathetic nervous system which releases different hormones into the system that gives feelings of euphoria and pleasure.

People that use this modality regularly report to be happier, have less muscle pain and soreness, and cope with stress more efficiently.

https://www.discovermagazine.com/health/the-science-behind-cold-water-plunges

https://www.healthline.com/health/cold-water-therapy

Chapter 49

Will You Scrape Me?

Sounds funny BUT I'm serious. We really don't ever pay attention to or address things that aren't major in the forefront of our minds. Therefore, we miss out on key things like muscle tension, stiffness, and thickened, knotted fascia. Fascia, the connective tissue that surrounds bones, nerves, organs, and muscles holding everything in place, is part of the human body that commonly goes overlooked. Over time, fascia can get stuck causing major stiffness in all areas of the body. Scraping, AKA Gua Sha, will help this.

In 2018, I learned about scraping and decided to go ahead and try my luck at what the process would do for me. After the pink quartz and jade tools I ordered arrived, I got to work. I tested the effectiveness of this modality by turning my head to the left and right to examine the range of movement before I scraped compared to the range of movement after I did the work. When I tell you I was floored at what a little scraping did for my mobility, I am not exaggerating.

I was able to move my head about two more inches to each side after I finished scraping. This amazed me so much, I wanted to identify what else my efforts could help.

Armed with my understanding of fascia and tightness in the body, I decided to try my tools out on a friend. For months, he had complained about lower back pain. Using some coconut oil and my jade tools, I began to scrape.

After about twenty minutes of working on the fascia from his lower back up to his neck, I told him to stand and check for any relief. He was amazed! The tightness in his lower back reduced significantly, and his mobility increased. This was not a placebo effect because he didn't believe that something so simple would make such a massive difference.

One last thing about scraping I observed in me personally was the emotional release I achieved. After every scrape session I gave myself, I would become emotional. From my study of trauma and trauma responses in the body, this made complete sense. Emotions are stored in the body, especially over time, when pushed down, ignored, and left unprocessed. When I loosened the tightness of the fascia around my body, the force also loosened the stored and locked emotions I gathered over the years. This support helped me process some of these emotions and finally let go. A very powerful and simple biohack.

https://www.healthline.com/health/beauty-skin-care/how-to-use-gua-sha

https://www.medicalnewstoday.com/articles/320397

Chapter 50

Red Light Isn't Just for Amsterdam

One of my ultimate favorite therapies! Red light therapy brought me to new, faster levels with my healing. When I learned about the therapy, I was so excited I ordered the first device I could get my hands on. Unfortunately, after thirty days of using the red light very little changed, but I did create a healthy pattern in my life of meditating in front of the light every morning.

This effort conditioned my body and mind to recognize that when I sit in front of red light therapy, or RLT, I am to relax and go into a meditative state. Since doing that every morning for weeks, my body naturally went into a calm and relaxed state as soon as I turned the light on. This happens to me still to this day.

Laying back during my red light therapy session. I look completely relaxed because I AM.

After deeper research, I found out that all lights are NOT created equal. I ended up buying a more expensive light from a trusted source, and all I can say is wow. After the first ten minutes under this new light, I recognized a difference between the two that I owned.

After a couple of days using the new light, I saw noticeable improvements. I became energetic, I got through my day with no lethargy, and I realized pain relief in my muscles and joints. I also noticed acne and fine lines diminish and my skin looked healthier and more vibrant. This is probably due to the stimulation of collagen production the light provides.

Red light activates the mitochondria in the body. Mitochondria, also known as the cell's powerhouse, produce adenosine triphosphate (ATP). ATP is what energizes the cells and keeps them functioning properly.

Scan the QR code and shop your Red Light Therapy device

I also noticed my HRV or Heart Rate Variability would spike during my sleep, with my HRV levels highly increased after evening sessions of RLT. A consistent increase in HRV overnight shows considerable physical recovery. This proved that by doing my red light therapy in the evenings, my body would have a better recovery throughout the night than when I didn't do a RLT session.

You're probably wondering how I was able to see my HRV increasing overnight. This goes into my next modality, the Oura Ring a wearable tracking device. I use my ring to track different biological reactions during the day and night within my system.

https://www.medicalnewstoday.com/articles/3-minutes-of-deep-red-light-can-improve-a-persons-vision

https://heliotherapy.institute/red-light-therapy-trials/#gref

https://www.theralight.com/theralight-case-studies/

Chapter 51

My Favorite Wearable Tracking System – Track with Style

Awareness is key when it comes to this healing journey. Awareness is NECESSARY when it comes to bio-hacking. The tools used by most all bio-hackers are wearable devices to provide measurements of simple biological functions like sleep states, number of steps, HRV, heart rate, and more. These devices come in all shapes and sizes, and I've owned most of them.

The Oura Ring is by far my favorite of the three devices I have used mainly because I can easily wear one on my finger, rather than a bulky bracelet on my wrist. They make different colors and they look nice! I found I like the smaller wearables better. I also receive superior readings from the Oura Ring, which makes sense, because a more accurate arterial reading is taken. This device gathers data using infrared light, instead of green light, which measures much deeper than green. I would not recommend green light for melonated skin types at all, as the readings are not accurate. The melanin in the skin absorbs the light instead of reflecting the measurement.

I love this ring because I am provided with so much awareness about my habits and routines. I can now measure if something affects my sleep in a negative or positive way because my ring takes those readings, I can see if my body has recovered enough to work out and obtain the most benefit possible, or if I should just take a day off and relax. Another feature I like about this ring is that I can "take a moment". The moment measures my heart rate, skin temp, and HRV which is great for doing self-checks during the day.

Sleep states are SO important for optimal mental and physical health. Good sleep, in general, may be the top thing needed for optimal mental and physical health. There are different levels of slumber we pass into throughout the night and each serve a specific purpose; achieving an adequate amount of each type per night is important. The body and brain heavily detox during our sleep and being able to "hack" it, to make us more efficient, is beneficial and necessary for healing.

Remember, awareness is key in regard to being a dedicated bio-hacker so we can manipulate and change things to become more optimal, which is why I will keep this ring for good on my bio-hacking journey

https://ouraring.com/

Chapter 52

Completely Free, and the Most Overlooked

Breathing correctly is at the top of the list of the most important bio-hacks one can accomplish during a lifetime. To breathe properly is LIFE. Breath is free in this life and yet many don't even pay attention to how we are breathing. The majority of people breathe very shallow, and they unconsciously hold their breath throughout their day, which is something I used to do.

Regarding breath, there were two profound moments in my life. One occurred after I put a grounding patch on my solar plexus. The other came when I was receiving body work that cleared inflammation in my gut. I took the deepest breaths I had ever taken in my life, and during those two breaths, I experienced what it was like to breathe life into my lungs.

When the gut is inflamed and our organs loop around each other becoming out of place, this highly affects every breath. When we clear that inflammation and get visceral body work done, profound positive change happens not only for physical health, but we finally are able to breathe the way we were meant to breathe—deeply.

Breathing is also effective in moving stagnant energy and emotion out of your system. When you are in a deeply emotional and reactive state—a stress response—you tend to automatically hold your breath. When you can become conscious of when your body goes into a stress response, and breathe deeply, the positive movement and flow of air actually processes, moves, and rids the body of stagnant energy and negative feelings.

There are many different styles of breathwork used these days and all serve unique purposes. My advice to anyone is to research and try many forms. All are free, many are easy, and we can even rise to greater states of enlightenment by using these varied techniques.

https://www.healthline.com/health/box-breathing

https://www.healthline.com/health/wim-hof-method

https://chopra.com/articles/how-breathwork-benefits-the-mind-body-and-spirit

Chapter 53

The Profound Effect of a Wooden Egg

In my Breath section, I wrote about inflammation in the gut. Another significant issue that can affect breathing is the hiatal hernia syndrome. Like me, tons of people have this issue to different degrees and don't even know.

The hiatal is a hole in the diaphragm, through which the esophagus passes to become the stomach. A hernia is a term that represents a weakened or torn muscle or fascia, where an organ then protrudes through the tissue. A hiatal hernia is when the stomach gets forced upwards into the diaphragm, which causes so many issues, the main one being a disruption to the vagus nerve.

The vagus nerve is the largest nerve in the body, and in my opinion, one of the most overlooked parts of our bodies. I wish they taught more about the correct stimulation of this nerve in schools because it directly influences how a person feels. You can greatly affect the sway between the sympathetic and parasympathetic shifts of your autonomic nervous system and bring the body back into homeostasis. Pulling the stomach down, releasing the hiatal hernia and freeing the impact on the vagus nerve benefits the body to have a more regulated nervous system.

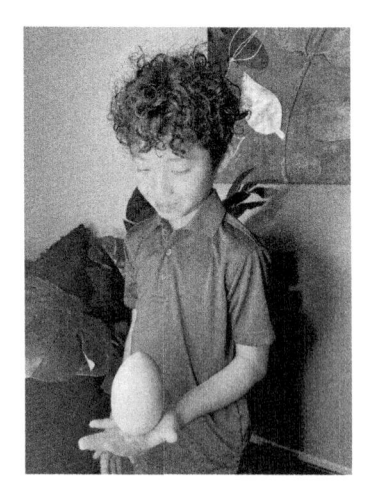

A hiatal hernia can be caused by many different reasons including the foods one eats, stress, physical and mental trauma, the weakening of surrounding muscles, and more. This issue also feeds into TONS of other symptoms like digestive difficulties, breathing and circulation problems, localized pain in random areas, headaches, mental stress, candida, menstrual or prostate problems, obesity, cravings for sugar, the list goes on and on.

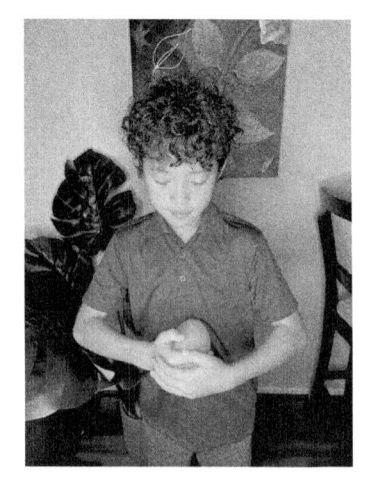

My 4-inch wooden egg

By taking my wooden tool, literally a 4-inch wooden egg, and pulling my stomach down, I changed my life! After implementing the practice three times a day—in the morning, afternoon, and evening—I breathed deeply all day, and the acid reflux I had dealt with pretty much my whole life, went away.

See how Gabriel holds the egg slightly to the left of the solar plexus. You push in the egg and pull down.

Because of this simple bio-hack, my digestion has improved. I can practically use any tool to simply pull my stomach down, but the wooden egg I found at a holistic wellness center works wonders.

An outstanding book to read about this issue is called "Hiatal Hernia Syndrome: The Mother of All Illness?" by Theodore A. Baroody, N.D., D.C., Ph.D

Chapter 54

The Nerve to Control My Mood

We touched on the vagus nerve a bit in the Wooden Egg section, but I definitely want to go a little deeper into the importance of great vagus nerve health. When the vagus nerve is stimulated, the heart and blood pressure calm down, and puts the body into a parasympathetic state. The vagus nerve can overreact which can lead to a very slow heart rate and fainting. This is known as vasovagal syncope. Let's just say that an underactive OR overactive vagus nerve can cause major issues thus the importance of vagus nerve health.

I have experienced anxiety that I became deeply aware of in the last four years. I can immediately tell if something pushes my nervous system into fight or flight now because I feel my heart speed up, hands get clammy, breath shorten, and I get a tickling sensation in my gut. Now, I know when my body goes into that state that I can stimulate my vagus nerve to down-regulate my system. I do this by pulling on my earlobe, taking a couple of fingers and stroking down my neck behind my ear, and focusing on deeper, slower, breaths.

This nerve is the main component of the parasympathetic nervous system. It's responsible for not only heart rate and blood pressure control, but also our moods, immune response, regulation of internal organ function, and digestion. This nerve is also named the "wanderer nerve" because of its length beginning in the brainstem going all the way down through the abdomen.

Find out more about the vagus nerve and how to keep it healthy:

https://patient.info/news-and-features/is-the-vagus-nerve-really-the-key-to-our-mental-health-and-well-being

https://www.ncbi.nlm.nih.gov/pmc/articles/PMC5859128/

https://www.healthline.com/human-body-maps/vagus-nerve

Chapter 55

The Best Kind of Heat

I love this modality for many reasons. Not only does the infrared sauna help my mental state, but I also additionally gain an incredible number of physical benefits. I started using the infrared sauna in 2017. Finding mixed research on the benefits of hot coal or wood saunas, I decided to use the infrared sauna because of the specific benefits this sauna provides. I speak from personal experience and preferability.

My experience in the infrared sauna is a mix between the mental and physical for me. I go into deep meditation or read a book every time I enter the sauna. Over time, because I have conditioned my body to do these things, my body promptly reacts to the environment and calms down without my need to consciously focus on the effort.

The difference between a hot wood/stone sauna and infrared is the heat level. Traditional saunas typically heat up to temperatures above 190 °F much higher than the heat needed to gain health benefits. The infrared sauna only needs to be heated to 120-150 °F to provide intense detoxification and sweating.

An infrared sauna uses light to heat the body through far-infrared rays. Infrared light also penetrates deeper into the layers of the body so detoxing occurs at a higher rate in these saunas. A traditional sauna heats our skin by warming the air around our bodies whereas the infrared sauna uses invisible rays of light that penetrate deep within our skin and heats us from the inside out.

Infrared saunas have so many benefits including faster muscle recovery, intense body detoxification, relief of tension, decreased inflammation in the body, increased circulation, enhanced weight loss, stimulated sweat glands, improved sleep, boost to the immune system, and much more.

https://www.ncbi.nlm.nih.gov/pmc/articles/PMC5505738/

https://www.healthline.com/health/infrared-sauna-benefits#What-is-an-infrared-sauna?

Chapter 56

Life Force Energy from the Universe

I mentioned how I have been interested in energy from an early age, so when I learned about Reiki I was immediately hooked. Reiki uses the cosmic, universal healing energy to balance and heal the physical, spiritual, and emotional body. There are different levels of Reiki practitioners ranging from beginner, intermediate, and master. Once the master level of Reiki is accomplished, the practitioner can attune and train others to practice.

For years, my good friend Valeria Palov has practiced Reiki and achieved the master level status. Since my energy system is not currently attuned to channel the cosmic energy of Reiki effectively, I asked my friend to perform the healing practice on me to gauge my reaction. The results blew me away.

To begin, she placed her hands on different parts of my body. As she did this, varied emotions came up, attached to different images presented in my head. When she finished and explained to me what she went through, it aligned exactly with what I felt during the session. My body and emotions gained a greater level of balance compared to what they held prior to the session. My friend found my left side blocked; the left side represents the feminine energy. She helped me remove that block, which successfully connected me to my divine feminine energy. I felt the change after the session, and its effects have been long-standing.

Another instance I recall involved a migraine. Nothing helped me. In desperation, my last effort, I called Valeria and asked for a remote Reiki session. Remote distance healing, or distance Reiki energy work, and can be done from anywhere. Since she lives in Florida and I live in Michigan, distance Reiki was my only option. She performed the session and I gained immediate relief. This practice works.

Luckily for me, Valeria is a reiki master, so she is able to attune people to it. In the future, I look forward to my own attunement, which allows me to perform Reiki!

Valeria Palov Instagram - @lovevaleria

https://www.ncbi.nlm.nih.gov/pmc/articles/PMC5871310/

https://clinicaltrials.gov/ct2/show/NCT00346671

Chapter 57

Sesame Oil, Body Love

I searched up the support of sesame oil after reading about Ayurveda medicine in a book by Deepak Chopra. In the Ayurveda practice, sesame oil has many benefits including stress reduction, improved sleep, and improved circulation. In addition, this oil is antibacterial, antifungal, and has anti-inflammatory properties, which makes the oil effective for internal uses like oil pulling. Sesame oil also promotes body strength, nourishes the bones and muscles, and is thought to lubricate the joints as well.

Not only did these physical benefits of this oil help me, but the mental benefits of addressing and rubbing each part of my body elevated my experience. After my shower, I would stand and gently rub sesame oil all over my body, all the while thanking each body part as I rubbed.

We don't take enough time to THANK our intelligent vessel that we live in during this life. I always had issues with self-esteem, and this body love practice was a game changer. My expression of gratitude for each part of my body developed in me a more confident attitude from the top of my head, all the way down to my pinky toe.

Become grateful for each part of our bodies as each part plays such an intelligent function. When we become grateful for our bodies, our bodies become grateful for us, and the alignment this creates within us is called, PEACE.

https://www.india.com/health/benefits-of-sesame-oil-for-health-and-skin-how-it-helps-in-digestion-and-becomes-a-warrior-for-your-skin-on-bad-days-5065035/

https://www.healthline.com/health/beauty-skin-care/sesame-oil-for-skin

https://www.ncbi.nlm.nih.gov/pmc/articles/PMC5796020/

Chapter 58

Address Your Mouth Piece

Oil pulling and tongue scraping are big in Ayurveda medicine, thought to improve bad breath, reduce inflammation and improve gum health, kill harmful bacteria, prevent cavities, and improve overall health. The mouth is the entry way to the digestive system. As the first point of entry, it is important to keep an eye on what enters our system this way.

I first read about oil pulling in a Deepak Chopra book called "Perfect Health". I heard about it again on a podcast I was listening to by well-known bio-hacker Ben Greenfield. He provided an oil pulling recipe using coconut oil, clove, and mint essential oil warmed and mixed together, then stored in the refrigerator overnight until hardened inside an ice cube tray or jello mold. This prep work provides easy access to oil pulling sessions. I have found over my years of bio-hacking that the less thought process going into these different modalities, the greater chance I had of trying and sticking with it.

When oil pulling came up for the second time, I decided it was time for me to try it. I made the mix that Ben Greenfield suggested and began to start the oil pulling process each morning. I found after doing this for a couple weeks that my teeth looked whiter, almost like I bleached them. I also experienced a reduction in previous gut issues that occasionally popped up. Oil pulling is something to highly consider incorporating into a daily routine. The overall benefits over time are life changing.

    https://www.ncbi.nlm.nih.gov/pmc/articles/PMC5198813/

    https://www.medicalnewstoday.com/articles/323757

Chapter 59

You Better Get to Scrubbing Your Skin

It would utterly surprise anyone to know how much filthy residue from clothing, soaps, lotions, dirt, and more is accumulated on our skin over the years. I came across a skin scrub through Dr. Robert Cassar of the Earther Academy. Having never specifically used a full-body skin scrub for pore detoxification and skin rejuvenation, I decided to go ahead and try it.

The Skin Scrub Recipe

- 1.75 liter Vodka in a glass bottle
- 2 tbsp of Diatomaceous Earth Fossil Shell Flour Food Grade
- 2 tbsp of Sodium Bicarbonate
- 2 tbsp of MSM Powder
- 2 tbsp of Liquid Himalayan Sole Salt or 1 Tbsp of Fine Ground Himalayan Salt.
- 2 tbsp of Ionic Magnesium with Trace Minerals
- 2 tbsp of Living Silica

This is the basic recipe for starting the skin and pore detoxification/rejuvenation protocols.

You also need:

- Coconut Oil
- Cacao Butter
- Wash Cloths

I mixed the ingredients and followed the directions from the website: https://eartheracademy.com/course/vodka-skin-cleaning-solution/

The first time I did this, I wanted to see what would come off my skin, so I used a pure, white towel to scrub. I went outside in the sun on a hot summer day and began to scrub my skin starting with my arms. What was coming off, blew me away. Not only did I see black coming off, but as I kept on scrubbing, I found blue AND red. The red was so bright I thought I scrubbed too hard and started to bleed.

After looking at my body and seeing no skin punctures, I thought for a moment and realized what the red and blue could have been from. Clothing! I wore jeans and a red top the day prior to my first-time scrubbing. The depth of color that came off my skin blew me away. The colors blue and red were as bright as if I threw dye on the towel.

When I processed what this scrub was taking off my skin, I realized how much toxic material gets absorbed into our bodies transdermally. Skin is the body's biggest organ and research says that 60% of anything that hits your skin gets absorbed straight into our systems. This is why it is so important to completely clean our skin beyond what a simple shower provides. Unfortunately, most body washes these days are toxic, full of parabens, BPA, triclosan, benzophenone-3, and more, and shouldn't be used anyway.

The results of using this scrub were a previously white towel turned multi-colored and tie-dyed, and a sense of weightlessness. I sat in the sun for a while and experienced how the sun's rays felt

The Recipe to Elevated Consciousness

different on my skin. With my pores cleaner than ever, I lay blanketed by comfort and warmth, which was unlike my previous experiences with the sun.

I continued the scrub every other day for some weeks until the white towel finally stopped turning different colors. Layers and layers of dye were scrubbed off my skin. When I worked out, my body sweated everywhere, which made sense with my newfound pore detoxification.

Scan this QR code to go to Earth Shift Products

Chapter 60

Play with My Organs – Body Work

There are parts of the body that people wouldn't even think to address. When we do not address different body parts, toxicity gets stuck, emotion gets stuck, inflammation is created, energy gets blocked, and much more. Visceral work is necessary because different parts of the body are associated with different emotional responses, working on these areas to help facilitate detoxification is important. For instance, the liver/gall bladder represents anger, kidneys/bladder-fear, lung/large intestine-sadness and depression, spleen/stomach pancreas-worry and anxiety, and heart/small intestine-hate and impatience.

Through body work, I achieve emotional releases. Everything I stuffed down in my life finds a way to come up. I have the most trouble with anger and anxiety/worry, which correlates with the liver and spleen. I find this correlation interesting and supportive because when I first started with body work, my liver and spleen were both very inflamed. The practitioner moved my organs in my body using a visceral manipulation therapy to free my liver and spleen. That evening and the next day I was extremely emotional and very angry. I was able to process through these stuck emotions in my system, and after I allowed myself to feel these uncomfortable emotions, I gained a deeper sense of awareness and peace.

Looking back over the past couple years of getting body work done, I can see the help it provided me. In the moment, the change this modality brings goes unrecognized, unless there is a major release of emotion during a session. But as I review my life and the different decisions I made following the work, I can see my growth and understand the contrast and benefit of the work. Moving my organs and releasing stuck inflammation and energy has created more space within my mind, body, and soul to become more aware and less reactive.

Chapter 61

A Flush Everyone Should Try

When I first learned of this modality, hydra colon therapy, I was terrified. They're going to do what??? A friend of mine who consistently uses colon cleanses, shared that it helps clear brain fog. Because I had a lot of residual issues from the drugs I did when I was younger, the idea sold me. Being me and willing to try anything once, I took a deep breath and scheduled my appointment.

Walking into the small office of this holistic care facility, I noticed the sweat on my hands. My body was obviously in sympathetic—fight or flight. Clearly, I feared what was to follow. The doctor welcomed me in, made me feel super comfortable, and shared the instructions for us to get the process started. I surrendered and he began.

While the water entered my colon, the doctor worked my gut to get the most out of the process. I bore the pressure, although slightly painful, because I knew the benefit greatly outweighed the discomfort. During the session, the doctor told me about clients who expelled visible parasites. This possibility freaked me out. Since the open system allowed me to see what came out of my colon, I kept a close eye out for any parasites.

Luckily, I didn't have any, but parasites are SO common. Signs that a person may have parasites are sugar cravings, mood swings, skin rashes, stomach cramps, weight loss, dehydration, muscle and joint pain, swollen lymph nodes, and digestive problems. It's estimated that 80% of adults and children have parasites.

After my cleanse, I could tell some of my brain fog cleared. I also felt lighter. Over time, old waste gets trapped in the colon, which causes all types of issues. I observed the difference from when I nervously walked into the facility to when I left. Even colors appeared brighter. I continue to regularly utilize cleanses, especially after traveling to different countries, to offset the higher risk of getting a parasite. There are many other reasons I keep consistent with this modality. These treatments keep my mind clear, my fear of getting parasites to a minimum, my body lighter, and an overall sensation of being cleaner.

Chapter 62

The Space Place

One of the most important, if not THE most important, modalities to practice daily is meditation. This one is also FREE! The addition of meditation to my life has unconditionally turned me around. Meditating calmed me down in all areas of my life. I used to overreact easier, to get triggered by more, and have my thoughts much more jumbled. Meditating turned these things around for me and created space for more awareness within my being.

After regularly practicing meditation, I started to have mystical experiences. I would connect to the universal experience of oneness. Within this dimension, I receive downloads that have helped my life enormously. It's very hard to explain these experiences using language, as language puts on parameters that confine the expression.

https://news.harvard.edu/gazette/story/2018/04/harvard-researchers-study-how-mindfulness-may-change-the-brain-in-depressed-patients/

The process of meditation can seem quite overwhelming within the busy lifestyle that we endure but start somewhere. If you don't make time for yourself, you'll end up either taking time off your life at the end, or your physical body will MAKE you make time for it. I prefer to take the time out for self care so I have lesser chances of being sick. Begin with one micro movement, then another, then another, which turns into a macro outcome. Once I began on a path to healing through these techniques, I didn't want to stop. We start to move closer to our divine nature, away from trauma responses and triggers. We start attracting what is truly meant for us as we clear our mind, body, and soul. Manifestation becomes almost immediate as one progresses on this healing journey.

Chapter 63

Thank You Thank You Thank You

Gratitude—a key ingredient to a happy and healthier life. I am so thrilled that I can now live my life with a deep sense of daily gratitude, but it wasn't always like this.

After I went through my last break-up with D, I was full of self-doubt, resentment, and hopelessness. I struggled to figure out a way to bring happiness back into my life. I realized that my thoughts were stuck in negative patterns, and I needed to get out of that to pull myself back together. I wanted to change my thought processes and looked for any means to assist my effort.

I read somewhere that upon waking, you should immediately write five things that you are grateful for and that the effort could change your thought patterns. Because I was stuck, this seemed like a great way to get started with scrapping those negative patterns. The second step of the method was to repeat the process directly before bed. Doing this creates new neural pathways in your brain. The two steps completed a cycle that helped the feeling of gratitude become automatic.

I was taken back by how quickly this process worked for me. I started seeing all the things and relationships I HAD instead of what

I DIDN'T have. My life became more hopeful. Not only did my mental life become brighter, but colors looked more vibrant, nature looked more beautiful, and things became wonderous. I returned to the child-like freedom of seeing the world through innocent eyes for the first time.

I suggest you start this practice and really become grateful for the goodness within your life as gratitude automatically attracts more abundance.

Chapter 64

The Key to Unlocking the Real Knowledge Within

These days it saddens me that I find kids interact with more screens than books. A study I read measured what the brain looks like in a child after playing on a screen for only fifteen minutes, and the results were shocking. The brain looked similar to the brain of an adult alcoholic. Think about this before you let your children use these devices for hours on end.

Books are a HUGE part of my healing growth. Something different happens when I open up a brand new book and really take in the words on the page. I probably read close to a hundred books in my first year while I explored my newfound consciousness. This amazing experience increased my knowledge base as well as expanded on what I already knew to be true.

Some of my favorite authors are Billy Carson, Wayne Dyer, Sadhguru, Gabrielle Bernstein, Ben Greenfield, Dr. Daniel Amen, Clint Ober, Esther and Jerry Hicks, Dave Asprey, Bruce Lipton, Brian L. Weiss, Deepak Chopra, Joe Dispenza, Eckhart Tolle, Brene Brown, Tony Robbins, and Oprah Winfrey. This is just to name a few that have stuck out throughout my path, but there are MANY more books to indulge in that add tremendous value.

Afterword

These days, I'm living within my purpose and manifesting my dreams into this reality. I've joyfully accepted myself as a master manifester, and I realize this reality is possible for everyone to achieve once they face their inner shadows.

All this is possible because of my belief in self. I am able to see the future I want, feel it in my body through emotion, and project my conscious thought waves outward until they return to me in form.

By the time the manifestation comes back to me, it honestly doesn't amaze me or make me FEEL any type of way. Having already created this feeling within me, knowing it was already mine, I receive it without surprise; rather, it is expected.

One of the major things that I've noticed about living my best life is the gaping hole I used to feel within my body of something missing is completely gone. I feel whole, powerful, conscious, and grateful. There is no remanence of the empty feeling that used to haunt me on a daily basis.

The reactiveness in me has diminished to where I am able to catch myself 99% of the time. My physical body doesn't get taken over with emotion attempting to control my consciousness anymore.

Afterword

Rather, my strong consciousness overpowers the emotion that may flood my body from a trigger.

This is huge!

I now have control over myself, AND my life. I may have a few slip-ups, like every human, as we are not perfect, but I can assure you I've come a LONG way.

I don't shoot at tires anymore because of road rage, I don't even have road rage. Imagine the HUGE amount of anger that must exist within someone to get mad enough to shoot at a stranger's tires. I don't even feel triggered by people driving recklessly anymore. Think about that for a second. That's a TON of anger cleared out of my physical form to go from that extreme to none at all.

Because I've done the work and continue to do so daily, I have attracted high vibrational beings into my life. I am surrounded by friends that are on the same path as me, people seeking the knowledge I have to offer and who can reciprocate the knowledge I need. My life is full of beautiful moments that exceed my expectations.

I am now in a healthy, loving relationship, with an amazing and brilliant being with the same goal as me—helping people around the world, and that's what we work to accomplish every single day. We live our best life every single day in gratitude and love, all the while creating and living in our purpose.

What more could I ask for?

Just in the past year, I've been to seven different countries vacationing AND working to expand my knowledge base. I've always wanted to travel the world and learn about different cultures, people, and hidden secrets that are found everywhere, and that's exactly what I'm currently doing and will continue to do. My life is my dream come true.

My beautiful son has grown into such an extraordinary being. Our relationship is stronger than ever, and for that, I'm so grateful. He has an emotional intelligence that is seen by all. He cares for and respects children and adults which I hear about all the time at our parent-teacher conferences. This fills my heart with joy, as I've

Afterword

always taught him how to handle his emotion and trauma so he doesn't have to hold on to things like I did throughout my life. My effort has paid off big time with him and is reflected in his maturity and interactions with others.

I attribute our successes to the modalities as well. He was right there next to me diving into these different therapies.

I am living proof that ANYONE, no matter the situation and no matter the trauma, CAN heal, CAN get free of negative self-soothing patterns, CAN feel better, and can feel COMPLETE.

It all starts with YOU and the belief in self.

All I can say is without keeping consistent with my self-care routines with these modalities, I would not be where I'm at today—healed from past traumas, free from the chains of drugs and alcohol, and bio-hacking my BEST life every day.

Take a leap of faith.

This is my recipe to elevated consciousness.

The Many Adventures of Elisabeth Hoekstra

Become the Co-Creator of your BEST life and instill more self awareness, address the stress and trauma that manifest physically in your vessel, and change your internal and external environments to live an optimal life.

Follow Elisabeth Hoekstra's Podcast as she shares each and every detailed step you need to achieve your personal success through BIO-HACKING Your Best Life.

Follow Elisabeth on social media while she travels to exotic, mystical locations!

An emerging author and educator in the field of wellness, be sure to join Elisabeth on her amazing journey and become a Master of Bio-Hacking Your Best Life!

https://www.elisabethihoekstra.com/

Scan this QR code for easy access to all of Elisabeth's social sharing.

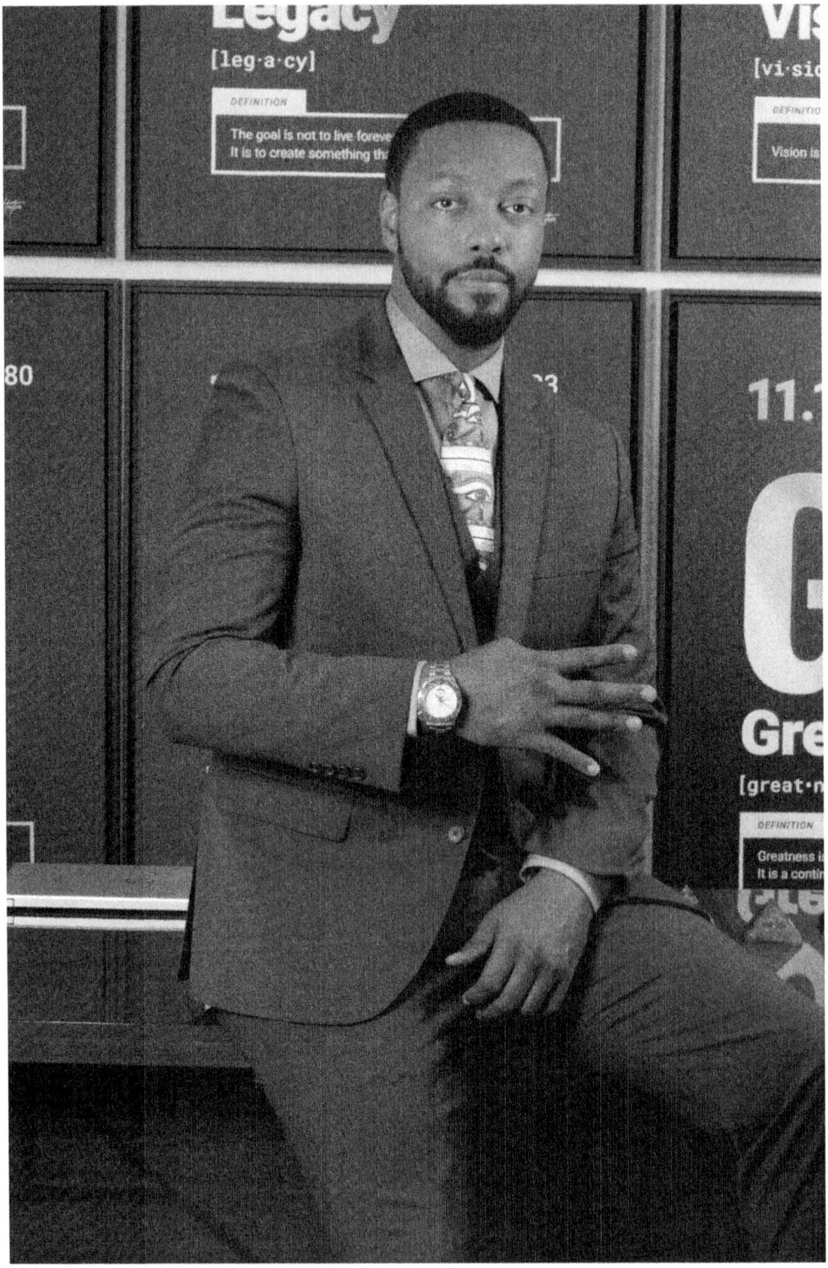

4BIDDEN 4BK KNOWLEDGE TV

Join the movement!

Become a part owner of 4biddenknowledge INC. Invest in an already fast-growing, profitable business. Be a founding member of a global streaming TV app platform that caters to fresh, alternative conscious content. Scan this QR code for the exciting details.

Scan the QR code to become a part owner of 4biddenknowledge INC.

Acknowledgments

Without a screen of support from those you count on, you would be lost in this life. We are social beings and NEED help from others. We NEED to connect. Connection is a bio-hack as the people you surround yourself with most affect your biology.

I am grateful for the abundance of people in my life that profoundly enhance my experience on this Earth. My girlfriends have stuck with me through thick and thin, two decades plus; I cannot thank them enough.

I am beyond grateful for my best friends Brittany, Jenay, Janell, and Rebecca. Each, throughout my life, were there to catch me when I fell.

Every exit I made from a terrible situation I found myself in was made with these women's loving words and support, my clan. These four kept me going as I saw the path of my journey. They held my hand when I wanted to die, inspired me to follow my dreams when I tried to give up, gave me the faith in myself to achieve when I had nothing to give myself.

Thank you. I can't say it enough, I love you all and thank you.

I've always had very strong male energies around me that have had my back, helped to protect my son and me, and have been loyal and respectful since the start. Just like you need a crew of girlfriends in life, I have always kept some of the same men around me—my brothers. I used to be more of a Tomboy when I was little, so getting along with men was always easier for me than getting along with women. Some of you guys have been family to me for over fifteen years and without all of your past and current support, I would not be the strong woman I am today. You all have taught me how to be independent, strong, and logical (something that's harder for women to be). You all have protected me in different ways when I was going through my crazy stage of life. Who knows, I might even be dead right now if it wasn't for some of you.

T.C. RIP, Treagen, Sal, Glen, HEX, Lemar, B, Bushman, I can't thank you all enough. I love you guys.

I want to acknowledge all the practitioners that have helped me on my journey. Each and every healer that I've come in contact with has either taught me or helped me become the best me I can be throughout every session I've experienced. Thank you Dawn, Dr. Perry, Mysteek, Ahmad, Dr. Berceli, Mindy, Dr. Jake, Valeria, Jason, Cortney… You all have added positively to my journey and helped me to become more aware and conscious. I couldn't have made it this far without each of you.

Inspiration in life comes in many forms. My appreciation for Billy Carson and the inspiration he gave me to write this book comes in only one—Gratitude. The thought of taking on the challenge of writing something like this had never really crossed my mind before meeting him. I always knew I wanted to share my story in some way, to help and inspire others, but I didn't see the direction that desire would take me.

One of the first things Billy told me after he heard the details of my story was, "Write the book." He told me to share where I had come from and the experiences I had grown through, that my life's story was one many needed to hear.

Billy, you inspired me to put myself out there and grind through the effort it takes to lay open and vulnerable enough to share something so deeply personal. Honestly, writing these details has healed something within me, and I owe that to you. You helped me stay positive and allowed me the space to get this done. Without you, there would be no "Recipe to Elevated Consciousness".

I love you and thank you.

I would love for you to enjoy these beautiful people as much as I do. Find them at:

 Billy Carson @4biddenknowledge
 Treagen @treagenkierstudios
 HEX @ironside.hex
 Bushman @bushmanonair
 Jenay @just_jenay
 Janell @innerbattlefitness
 Perry Nickelston @stopchasingpain
 Cortney @cortneykanesidesmedium
 Valeria @lovevaleria
 Mysteek @lymph.nymph
 Lemar @lemarjphoto

Index

Acupuncture 88, 139

Anger 13, 16, 85, 88, 121
    Boundaries 129
    Craniosacral Body Work 189
    Embrace Emotions 145
    SomatoEmotional Release Body Work 121

Anti-Inflammatory, Antibacterial, Antifungal 181

Anxious, Anxiety 79, 83, 100, 105, 153, 175
    Acupuncture 139
    Embrace Emotions 147
    Trauma Release Exercise 134

Apollo Neuro Wearable Device 141

Autonomic Nervous System 143, 173

Index

Ayurveda 181, 183

Balance 63, 79, 80, 83, 86, 91, 94
    Neurofeedback 111
    Reiki 179
    TRE, Trauma Release Exercise 133

Ben Greenfield 183

Body Scrub 185

Boundaries 129

Brain 17, 45, 66, 76, 79, 91, 96, 107
    Brain Fog 112, 191
    Brain Tap 137
    EFT, Emotional Freedom Technique 135
    Floatation Therapy 119
    Healing Relationships 131
    Heart Math 143
    Neurofeedback 111
    Oura Ring 170
    Talk Therapy 125

Breath, Breathe 5, 11, 45, 93
    Breath 171
    Grounding 115
    Heart Math 144
    Oil Pulling 183
    Psilocybin 150
    Vagus Nerve 175
    Wooden Egg 173

Index

Calm, Calming 13, 94
    Acupuncture 139
    Brain Tap 138
    Grounding 115
    Infrared Sauna 177
    Meditation 193
    Neurofeedback 111
    Red Light Therapy 167
    TRE, Trauma Release Exercise 133
    Vagus Nerve 175

Cellulite 161

Circulation 159, 161, 163, 174, 177, 181

Cleanse 158, 161, 185, 191

Cold Plunging 163

Cravings 139, 174, 192

Deepak Chopra 57, 183, 197

Detox 48, 108, 170, 177, 185, 189

Device
    Apollo Neuro 141
    Brain Tap 137
    EMDR, Eye Movement Desensitization and Reprocessing 155
    Grounding 115
    Heart Math 143
    Oura Ring 169
    Red Light Therapy 167

Index

Digestive, Digestion 174, 176, 183, 192

Disassociation 29, 121, 145

Dr. Robert Cassar 185

Dry Brushing 161

Earthing 115

Emotion, Emotional 4, 41, 68, 84
    Body Work 189
    Breath 171
    Embrace Emotions 145
    EFT, Emotional Freedom Technique 135
    Energy Vampires 151
    EMDR, Eye Movement Desensitization and Reprocessing 155
    Healing Relationships 131
    Negative Soothing 153
    Psilocybin 149
    Protect Yourself 129
    Reiki 179
    Scraping 166
    SomatoEmotional Release 121
    TRE, Trauma Release Exercise 133

Emotional Freedom Technique, EFT 133

Energy 37, 50, 61, 79, 81, 82, 86, 92, 93, 95, 97, 99
    Apollo Neuro 141
    Body Work 189
    Breath 171
    Cold Plunge Lymphatic 163

Index

    Embrace Emotions 146
    EFT, Emotional Freedom Technique 135
    Energy Vampires 151
    Grounding 116
    Heart Math 144
    Lymphatic Massage 158
    Rebounding 159
    Reiki 179
    SomatoEmotional Release 121
    TRE, Trauma Release Exercise 134

Eye Movement Desensitization And Reprocessing, EMDR 7, 155

Fascia 165, 173

Fight or Flight 80, 115, 143, 145, 175, 191

Floatation Therapy 88, 119

Grounding 83, 93, 115, 139, 171

Gua Sha 165

Healing 21, 79, 84, 87, 94, 97, 101, 107
    Boundaries 129
    Energy Vampires 151
    Grounding 115
    Healing Relationships 131
    Meditation 194
    Oura Ring 169
    Psilocybin 149
    Red Light Therapy 167
    Reiki 179

Index

    SomatoEmotional Release 121
    TRE, Trauma Release Exercise 133

Heart Math 143

Hiatal Hernia 173

Hydra Colon Cleanse 191

Inflammation
    Body Work 189
    Breath 171
    Dry Brushing 161
    Grounding 115
    Infrared Sauna 178
    Oil Pulling and Tongue Scraping 183
    Wooden Egg 173

Infrared Sauna 177

Light
    Brain Tap 137
    Floatation Therapy 119
    Infrared Sauna 177
    Lightning, Grounding 115
    Oura Ring 169
    Red Light Therapy 167

Lymph, Lymphatic 92, 157, 159, 161, 163, 192

Magnesium 108, 119, 185

Melonated Skin 169

Index

Muscle
    Cold Plunge 164
    Hydra Colon 192
    Infrared Sauna 178
    Red Light Therapy 167
    Scraping 165
    Sesame Oil 181
    Wooden Egg 173

Neurofeedback 75, 79, 83, 111

Oil Pulling and Tongue Scraping 183

Oura Ring 168, 169

Parasympathetic
    Grounding 115
    Heart Math 143
    Vagus Nerve 175
    Wooden Egg 173

Photobiomodulation 167

Post-Traumatic Stress Disorder, PTSD
    TRE, Trauma Release Exercise 133
    EMDR, Eye Movement Desensitization and Reprocessing 155

Practitioner Assisted
    Acupuncture 139
    Body Work 189
    EMDR, Eye Movement Desensitization and Reprocessing 155
    Hydra Colon 192
    Lymphatic Massage 158
    Neurofeedback 111

Index

    Reiki 179
    SomatoEmotional Release 121
    Spiritual Advisor 127
    Talk Therapy 125
    TRE, Trauma Release Exercise 133

Psilocybin 149

Rebounding 159

Red Light Therapy 167

Reiki 179

Relationships 23, 37, 54, 63, 66, 76, 88
    Boundaries 129
    Healing Relationships 131

Release 84, 88
    Body Work 189
    Boundaries 130
    Healing Relationships 131
    Scraping 166
    SomatoEmotional Release 121
    TRE, Trauma Release Exercise 133

Reprogram
    EFT, Emotional Freedom Technique 136
    EMDR, Eye Movement Desensitization and Reprocessing 155
    Floatation Therapy 119

Sauna, Infrared 177

Scraping

Index

    Gua Sha 165
    Tongue Scrapping 183

Sesame Oil 181

Skin
    Apollo Neuro 141
    Dry Brushing 161
    Floatation Therapy 119
    Grounding 116
    Hydra Colon 192
    Infrared Sauna 178
    Oura Ring 169
    Scrub 185

Sleep
    Apollo Neuro 141
    Grounding 115
    Infrared Sauna 178
    Oura Ring 169
    Red Light Therapy 168
    Sesame Oil 181

SomatoEmotional Release 121

Spiritual Advisor 127

Sympathetic
    Cold Plunge 164
    Grounding 115
    Heart Math 143
    Hydro 191
    Wooden Egg 173

Index

Talk Therapy 125

Tension
    Infrared Sauna 177
    Scraping 165
    TRE, Trauma Release Exercise 133

Tongue Scraping 183

Toxic
    Body Scrub 186
    Body Work 189
    Energy Vampires 151
    Lymphatic Massage 157

Trauma
    Boundaries 129
    Embrace Emotions 145
    EFT, Emotional Freedom Technique 136
    Energy Vampires 151
    EMDR, Eye Movement Desensitization and Reprocessing 155
    Healing Relationships 131
    Meditation 193
    Neurofeedback 111
    Psilocybin 149
    Scraping 165
    SomatoEmotional Release 121
    Spiritual Advisor 127
    Talk Therapy 125
    TRE, Trauma Release Exercise 133
    Wooden Egg 174

Trauma Release Exercise, TRE 133

Index

Vagus Nerve 173, 175

Vampires 151

Weight Loss
    Hydra Colon 192
    Infrared Sauna 178

Wooden Egg 173

Index Links

Acupuncture
https://theacademyofacupuncture.com/clinical-case-studies/
https://pubmed.ncbi.nlm.nih.gov/28483186/

Apollo Neuro
https://apolloneuro.com/pages/science

Brain Tap
https://braintap.com/

Breath
https://www.healthline.com/health/box-breathing
https://www.healthline.com/health/wim-hof-method
https://chopra.com/articles/how-breathwork-benefits-the-mind-body-and-spirit

Emotional Freedom Technique—EFT, Aka Tapping
https://www.healthline.com/health/eft-tapping
https://www.ncbi.nlm.nih.gov/pmc/articles/PMC6381429/

EMDR, Eye Movement Desensitization and Reprocessing
https://www.healthline.com/health/emdr-therapy

Floatation Therapy

Index Links

https://www.healthline.com/health/sensory-deprivation-tank
https://www.myfloatzone.com/casestudy

Grounding/Earthing

https://www.dovepress.com/the-effects-of-grounding-earthing-on-inflammation-the-immune-response--peer-reviewed-fulltext-article-JIR

https://earthinginstitute.net/wp-content/uploads/2016/07/Cortisol-Study.pdf

Heart Math

https://www.heartmath.com/science/

Infrared Sauna

https://www.ncbi.nlm.nih.gov/pmc/articles/PMC5505738/

https://www.healthline.com/health/infrared-sauna-benefits#What-is-an-infrared-sauna?

Lymphatics Cold Plunging

https://www.discovermagazine.com/health/the-science-behind-cold-water-plunges

https://www.healthline.com/health/cold-water-therapy

Lymphatics Dry Brushing

https://health.clevelandclinic.org/the-truth-about-dry-brushing-and-what-it-does-for-you/

Lymphatics Massage

https://www.livescience.com/26983-lymphatic-system.html
https://www.stopchasingpain.com/

Lymphatics Rebounding

https://cellercise.com/about-cellercise/

Neurofeedback

https://www.ncbi.nlm.nih.gov/pmc/articles/PMC4892319/
https://www.ncbi.nlm.nih.gov/pmc/articles/PMC4892322/

Oil Pulling and Tongue Scraping

https://www.ncbi.nlm.nih.gov/pmc/articles/PMC5198813/
https://www.medicalnewstoday.com/articles/323757

Oura Ring

Index Links

https://ouraring.com/

Red Light Therapy, AKA Photobiomodulation

https://www.medicalnewstoday.com/articles/3-minutes-of-deep-red-light-can-improve-a-persons-vision

https://heliotherapy.institute/red-light-therapy-trials/#gref

https://www.theralight.com/theralight-case-studies/

Reiki

https://www.ncbi.nlm.nih.gov/pmc/articles/PMC5871310/

https://clinicaltrials.gov/ct2/show/NCT00346671

Scraping, AKA Gua Sha

https://www.healthline.com/health/beauty-skin-care/how-to-use-gua-sha

https://www.medicalnewstoday.com/articles/320397

Sesame Oil body love

https://www.india.com/health/benefits-of-sesame-oil-for-health-and-skin-how-it-helps-in-digestion-and-becomes-a-warrior-for-your-skin-on-bad-days-5065035/

https://www.healthline.com/health/beauty-skin-care/sesame-oil-for-skin

https://www.ncbi.nlm.nih.gov/pmc/articles/PMC5796020/

Skin/Body Scrub

https://eartheracademy.com/course/vodka-skin-cleaning-solution/

https://news.harvard.edu/gazette/story/2018/04/harvard-researchers-study-how-mindfulness-may-change-the-brain-in-depressed-patients/

SomatoEmotional Release Body Work

https://www.healthline.com/health/mind-body/how-to-release-emotional-baggage-and-the-tension-that-goes-with-it#How-to-release-emotions-from-the-body

https://www.ncbi.nlm.nih.gov/pmc/articles/PMC5518443/

Spiritual Advisor

https://cortneykanesides.com

Trauma Release Exercise—TRE

https://traumaprevention.com/
https://www.ncbi.nlm.nih.gov/pmc/articles/PMC4268601/

Vagus Nerve

https://patient.info/news-and-features/is-the-vagus-nerve-really-the-key-to-our-mental-health-and-well-being

https://www.ncbi.nlm.nih.gov/pmc/articles/PMC5859128/

https://www.healthline.com/human-body-maps/vagus-nerve

Suggested Books:

Perfect Health by Deepak Chopra

Hiatal Hernia Syndrome: The Mother of All Illness? by Theodore A. Baroody, N.D., D.C., Ph.D

Printed in Great Britain
by Amazon